ROOK MAKES A MOVE

ROOK
MAKES
a move

a novel

CYNTHIA HILLIARD

Spindlewood
PRESS

Book Cover and Interior Design by VMC Art & Design LLC

Spindlewood Press
Pittsboro, NC

Published in the United States of America

ISBN: 978-1-7351936-0-1
LCCN: 2020910765

For David, my lion,
and for T & Q
... fingerends

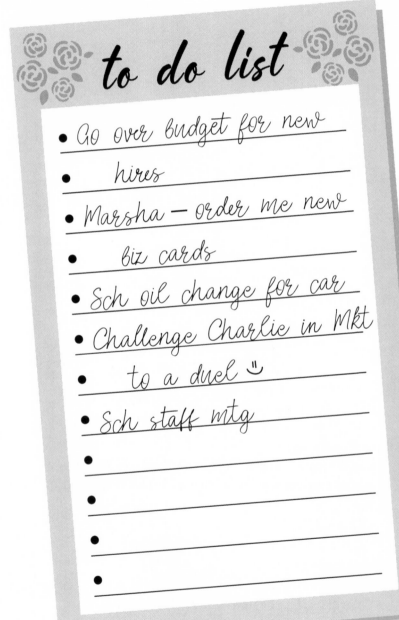

to do list

- Go over budget for new
- hires
- Marsha — order me new
- biz cards
- Sch oil change for car
- Challenge Charlie in Mkt
- to a duel ☺
- Sch staff mtg
-
-
-
-

CHAPTER ONE

January
Crossroads

Max changes everything.

My grandson's arrival has pulled my logical and rational approach to life out of kilter. In my sixty-one years on this earth, I've developed highly honed skills of analysis, problem-solving, and decision-making, but Max put a match to that. He ignited a fire that's burned down my worldview. Sure, I've fallen hard before and experienced that head-over-heels, giddy, reckless feeling familiar to anyone in love.

This is different.

This is compelling, intense, and beguiling. I now get the meaning of smitten.

This calls for action.

Max lives *there,* and I live *here*. It's untenable.

Picturing the events that have led to this point, I see my son, Jay. He is handsome in his tux, exchanging vows with Carly. Campbell and I look at each other through tears. Our bird has flown the nest and built one of his own.

Years later, Campbell and I each hold an ear to the kitchen phone to hear Jay's voice reaching us across the miles. "Carly's pregnant!" We whoop and grin, astounded—seven years since their wedding. The prospect of grandchildren had faded. We'd become content with our family of four.

A sonogram. I study it but can't, as my mother used to say, *make heads or tails of it.* Literally. I can't make out where the baby's head is, but I'm engulfed with a rush of love for the swirls of my future grandchild's anatomy.

Then, another phone call. Campbell and I play tug-of-war with the phone as Jay announces the arrival of Max on November 8, 2006. Seven pounds, eleven ounces, of perfection.

Now, Max takes center stage. Max smiling. Max rolling over. Max crawling. Max babbling. What you don't see in this production is me. The paternal grandmother. There are glimpses, but mostly I'm off stage. Part of the crew, rushing in between acts.

I envision a final scene: Max showing his grandchildren family photos. "Who's that?" pipes up an adorable blonde moppet, pointing. Max taps my picture. "That? That's my grandmother on my father's side. I didn't know her very well. I don't remember much about her."

I consider my legacy. Do I want to be remembered as an outstanding project manager? Reliable employee? No-nonsense team player? Or the grandmother with the best cookies?

Unparalleled read-aloud skills? Snuggliest bear hugs? Are these two visions of my legacy mutually exclusive?

They are, I decide. The geography of the situation demands a choice. I've tried the long-distance relationship thing: seeing Max every six to eight weeks for a long weekend. My frequent flyer balance is growing, but so is my dissatisfaction with the status quo.

I can hear what Campbell will say: "I love my job here. We're seeing Max all the time. Moving is huge. What if we move there and then Jay or Carly gets a new job somewhere else? Are we going to follow them around the country like puppy dogs?"

Yes. Woof.

The thing is, I love my job too. Well, I like it a lot. I like most everything about my life here in Ohio. We've got things down pat. We know the traffic shortcuts, which bakery has the best rolls, and what hardware store to trust. We have family, friends, and an amazing church community. We have roles to play and responsibilities to fulfill. We have roots here, a support network, and we just planted fifty lily bulbs in the yard. Moving is insane.

Yet, I can't help my mind drifting back to Max, showing the family photos to his grandchildren in sixty years with a different twist. Blonde moppet points, but this time Max says, "That? That's my father's mother. My Gram. I adored her."

I like this version of history, but I'm also a pragmatist. I have to figure out how to make sense of uprooting ourselves and moving halfway across the country. *How do I convince others (e.g., Campbell) that Rook McFadden hasn't lost it?*

Inspiration strikes. It's time to use my business skills.

I've been to dozens of classes in my banking career: Effective Decision-Making. Leadership. Overcoming Obstacles. Team-Building. Process Improvement. System Design. I'll apply proven techniques, which should reveal and support the right answer.

And if they don't?

That's why they invented do-overs.

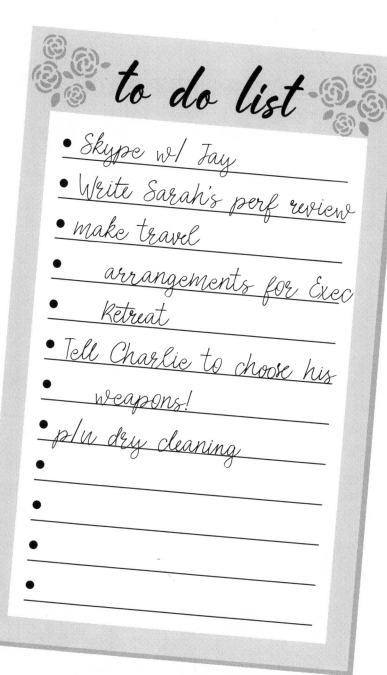

to do list

- Skype w/ Jay
- Write Sarah's perf review
- make travel
- arrangements for Exec
- Retreat
- Tell Charlie to choose his
- weapons!
- p/u dry cleaning

CHAPTER TWO

January

Seesaw

My mind is all over the place.

I spot a cruller in the break room as I pour myself a cup of coffee. I reach for it but stop when my inner beat-cop voice commands: *"Step away from the doughnuts, Ma'am. Nothing to eat here."*

Terry, from the Commercial Loan support group, comes in. "Hi, Rook," he says, and the dance begins. We're both new grandparents. Terry's daughter lives here, and he sees little Sophia often. My entry in the grandparent sweepstakes lives in Colorado. In my humble opinion, Max is cuter and smarter than Sophia, but distance puts me at a serious disadvantage when it comes to bragging rights for family outings.

"Did you see Sophia this weekend?"

"Yep. Took her to the aquarium." Terry pulls out his

phone, crammed with new pictures of Sophia, and I gush appropriately.

"Oh, she's so cute. What a wonderful smile." Picking up my coffee, I retreat to my corner office, knowing it trumps Terry's space in the cubicle farm. At least I've got him bested when it comes to corporate real estate.

When I take a seat at my desk, I see the photo of Max on my shelf. His adorable face reminds me that if I want to win at the grandparent game, it's all about location, location, location. Could I lure Jay and Carly back to the Midwest? The idea withers instantly. They're bonkers about where they live: the weather, the outdoors, the craft beers.

Since I don't have any meetings scheduled for the rest of the afternoon, I grant myself some personal time to think about my conundrum. Project Max. With a new determination, I let the noises of the busy office around me—phones, printers, footsteps, conversation, laughter—fade away.

What am I feeling right now? Usually, I ask myself: What's the *right* thing to do? The moral thing? The ethical thing? The legal thing? The logical thing? The Christian thing? Feelings have nothing to do with it. Suck it up and do what's required, considerate, appropriate, and mature. If I can work out a compromise that gets everyone a little of what they want, all the better. But feelings? *My* feelings? Not in the mix.

My emotions are running the gamut in my head. I am being bombarded with sadness, jealousy, a smidge of anger at Jay and Carly for living twelve hundred miles away, and resentment toward Campbell's contentment with the current situation. No wonder I don't consult my feelings. They're a disorganized mess.

I pick up my favorite rollerball pen and doodle on the

legal pad positioned in the middle of the blotter on my tidy desk. I draw a fairly recognizable cat, a house with a tree, and a snowman. I print my initials, then write them in a flowery script. I draw Charlie, my archrival at work, with large ears and a droopy mustache.

Time to get to work. I tear off my doodles, draw a line down the middle of a clean sheet of paper, print OHIO at the head of the left column, COLORADO on the right, and list the positives for each.

Ohio	Colorado
1. Good jobs	1. More sun
2. Nice house	2. More son — ha!
3. Great church	3. More g'son — yay!
4. Lifelong friends	
5. Family — Bishop. Howard. C's parents. etc.	

Stupid list. This uncharacteristic thought gets my attention. I love lists.

I stand and walk over to my window, which frames the full gloom of a January afternoon in Ohio. Snowflakes make a half-hearted attempt to accumulate, but the temperature is thirty-three degrees, and, like me, they are in a state of flux.

Do they want to be rain, sleet, or snow? Do I want to be logical or emotional? I know I'm playing mind games rather than figuring things out. *Ugh.* I can hear Campbell's advice: "Quit admiring the problem."

There's one factor I keep ignoring. Money. The song says money can't buy me love. But, maybe it can buy me Max. And Jay. And Carly. I need to get serious, sharpen my pencil, and figure out the financial aspects of a move. I love my son and his family, but we can't move in with them. Thanks to our two salaries, Campbell and I have come to enjoy our—*what's the saying?* Our upwardly mobile lifestyle. *Would moving shoot major holes in our retirement dreams? Do we even want to retire?* I'm pretty sure Campbell doesn't, and I'm not wild about the idea. I like working. But I love Max. *What's the employment situation in Colorado? What if only one of us were working? Do houses cost a lot more in Colorado? Would our house sell quickly?*

These thoughts chase each other around in my head until I feel a little queasy. There are big decisions ahead, and I don't have a compass to point me in the right direction. I pull out my corporate directory and call Phil in HR. He's helped me through the years with any number of sticky personnel issues.

"Hey, Rook. What's up?"

"Phil, hi. Quick question: When can I start drawing on my 401(k)?"

"Tax law says you have to be fifty-nine and a half to withdraw and not incur a financial penalty, except for taxes. I won't ask your age, but you are undoubtedly *waaay* too young."

Phil's shoveling BS, but I'm not made of stone, so I enjoy his flattery. I *can* withdraw, but should I? I plan on living to one hundred, so my retirement fund has to last a long time. I flash on an image of Campbell and me living in a studio apartment. Dipping into the candy jar this soon might not be a good idea, and Social Security isn't enough, even if I take it early. Campbell could draw his pension, but his Social Security will be substantially reduced because of his years in the public sector when he didn't pay into it. I'll have to crunch the numbers and call Bob Hale, our financial adviser, to see if we can maintain the manner to which we have become accustomed.

"Just considering my options, Phil. Thank you kindly."

I return to my list and read through it one more time. Then, I tack on another pro to each column.

Ohio	Colorado
1. Good jobs	1. More sun
2. Nice house	2. More son — ha!
3. Great church	3. More g'son — yay!
4. Lifelong friends	4. Mountains!!!
5. Family — Bishop. Howard. C's parents. etc.	
6. Growing our retirement income	

I call Phil again.

"Yas," he drawls. "How may I be of service?"

"Phil, how many sick days have I accumulated? What are they worth?"

"You *are* planning a runner." I hear his keyboard clicking. "Wow. Impressive. Do you ever take a day off?"

No, I don't. *Work, for the night is coming.* I hum the hymn to myself while Phil clicks.

"You have accumulated one hundred sixty-four sick days. That's the good news."

Now I hear Phil turning pages in a manual. I picture him hunched over a dusty book entitled *Crushing Employees' Dreams, Edition 14.*

"What's the bad news?"

"Company policy caps the payout for sick days at sixty days. So if you were sick, you could use all one hundred sixty-four. But if you leave and want a payout? You'd lose… wow… one hundred and four days' pay."

"OK, Phil. Thanks." I hang up and growl in irritation. *Damn. Double damn.*

I try some quick math. The sick day payout isn't going to help much. A moving van alone is what… $10,000? More? I start a new "To Do" list and put, "Get moving van estimate," as the first item. If I'm going to convince Campbell, I need to prove we can afford this move without impacting budget items he considers vital to his happiness. *And we all know what those are: new cars, bespoke suits, custom shirts, ever-larger TVs.*

I look around my office. I've decorated it to my taste, and within its walls, I operate with authority and precision. I manage people, projects, money, deadlines, and outcomes. I like my world here inside the bank, but for the first time, I see myself walking out. No regrets. Well…

Regrets? I've Had A Few…

** Never got to ride in the company jet
** Won't see the finish of the retail project
** Won't get to fire that weasel Carl
** Won't get a big retirement party

I look over at my bookcase again, at Max's picture. He's smiling, and his thought is as plain as the nose on his cute little face.

"Gram, those regrets? They are… too few to mention."

to do list

- Write quarterly rpt
- Invite Bishop/Barb to
  dinner
- Marsha — get me a new
  desk chair
- Charlie — Conf Rm 401
  — dawn
- Think up acronym for
  new credit card sys
-
-
-

CHAPTER THREE

January

Aha

P roject Max has killed my productivity.

At 4 p.m., I pack up. I'll go home early and have a cup of tea before Campbell gets home, with maybe, perhaps, possibly, just a tiny little cookie.

In the lot, I discover that someone has positioned their colossal truck over the dividing line, reducing access to my door to twenty inches. Campbell's name for this maneuver is the "truck you." I curse, wheeze, and wriggle my way in. I wonder if I could score a short commute if I moved to Colorado. Or no commute. *Sure*, says my brain, dripping sarcasm. *Maybe you could live in a candy cane house, too. Under a marshmallow sky.*

I head home in the fading light of a late winter afternoon. Project Max is resisting my usual techniques. My brain tells me there is only one logical conclusion, one bottom line that makes sense: continue living here and visit Max every chance we can.

Don't listen to that party pooper. You know you want to go. Do it!

My heart is proposing this rebellious notion, and I square off against it.

"But what about, you know, money?" I scold.

For once in your life, take a risk. My heart, if it had a finger, would be wagging it at me. *Where's your faith?*

I realize I've been driving on autopilot and, looking up, see a constellation of brake lights.

Are you kidding me? I never go home early, and today there's a traffic jam?

Hemmed in by cars and rumbling trucks, I roll to a stop and stare at the back of an eighteen-wheeler for ten minutes before an idea starts to take shape. With a central resolution and two opposing sides, Project Max is perfect for the debate format. It may have been a long time ago, but I was on my college debate team for two years and can still argue a point with the best of them, even if it is with myself.

First, I set the resolution:

RESOLVED: The McFaddens move to Colorado to be near their grandson.

I assemble the teams, although there's only one member per side. My heart is arguing the affirmative, my brain the negative.

My heart, at the podium, consults notes.

"Good afternoon, Madam. The affirmative team supports the resolution as stated. My first, and only, argument is this: Love trumps all. Thank you."

My brain goes next and constructs a magnificent negative case. Logical arguments. Clear delivery. Impeccable research. All the bullet points I wrote down in my office, plus new ones.

My heart, unperturbed, offers a rebuttal. *"In the end, family is what matters."*

I inch forward a few feet, still caught in the vise of traffic. The affirmative case is sentimental and not supported by facts, yet it's oddly compelling. My gut is urging the win be awarded to the opposition, but I resist.

I read once that if you can't make a decision, you should toss a coin and observe your first reaction to the result. Chance has delivered the answer. How do you feel? Disappointed? Pleased? Angry? Your emotion will reveal your true desire.

Does becoming a grandmother turn on some kind of emotional faucet? I'm not sure, but for the second time today, I take my emotional temperature. How do I feel? Sad. Plain and simple. I'm sad at the prospect of living here, despite my comfortable life, because Max is not here.

My dad used to say he'd "rather be right than President." I'm one hundred percent behind that idea, but figuring out the next right step in Project Max is proving difficult. My usual ways of figuring out a problem—profit and loss, decision trees, diagrams, models, theory—are all useless.

I bow my head. "Lord, I'm not looking for a sign, like the word 'Colorado' on the next billboard. I'm just asking for wisdom. Should the McFaddens stay here in Ohio or start a new chapter out west?"

Traffic begins to flow, and we pass an accident scene. Fascinated by the drama, my fellow motorists and I rubberneck our way past.

I *want* to move to Colorado. I *should* stay here. I *need* to be near Max. I *ought* to be sensible. "Screw it," I announce. Something bursts inside me, like the last set piece at a Fourth of July fireworks show. *Ooh. Aah.* Gorgeous streams of light shower down, illuminating, thrilling, proclaiming, "This is it, folks. The grand finale. What you've been waiting for."

Just like that, my heart wins. The McFaddens are moving.

As we like to say in the project management world, Project Max now has a final deliverable. Campbell and I will be living in Colorado. I can handle the pesky little details, like jobs and money. Getting Campbell to agree? All in good time.

It's like a line of dominoes. I see them stretching from central Ohio to the front range of Colorado. It's going to take a while to line them up, but once in place, and I tip over the first tile?

The result is inexorable.

to do list

- Bring home the bacon
- Fry it up in a pan
- Set up client roundtable
-     mtg
- Sign up — altar flowers
-     at church
-
-
-
-
-
-

CHAPTER FOUR

January

Battlefield

I skip the tea and cookie.

Once home, there's barely time to change and feed Sammie, our six-pound dorkie, a Yorkshire terrier/dachshund mix. By *our*, I mean *my*. Campbell is not a fan. "Too yippy," in his opinion. I like a small dog, one I can carry around and tuck in beside me. A lap dog.

"Instead, you've got a yap dog." His standard wisecrack.

The irony is that Sammie adores Campbell. She's always prancing at his feet, begging to be picked up. Playing hard to get must work. The more he ignores her, the more she pines for his attention.

She does have one infuriating habit. She barks at everyone who comes near the house, including Campbell, and me. That makes her a good watchdog, if a dog that weighs about the same as a sack of flour could do much damage to a trespasser. I've tried various methods to curb her barking, but none of them worked, so we live with it. *Some more graciously than others,* I observe to myself, as I scoop Sammie up for a cuddle.

I hear the garage door, and Campbell comes in, Sammie dancing in circles, barking. He tells her to "shut the hell up" and puts his briefcase and travel coffee mug down. He deposits a chocolate bar on the kitchen island.

"Gift from a parent," he says, looking remarkably energized, given he spent the day in the company of four hundred and eighty-two elementary school kids.

He points to a spot on his shirt. "Sorry. A second grader spilled pudding on me."

"Put it on the washer. I'll soak it. Any other disasters today, Principal McFadden?"

"Let's see. The teachers don't like the schedule. A fourth grader brought a knife to school. I had to give a kid his insulin shot. So—just routine." He grins. He loves his work.

I watch my husband as he dabs water on his shirtfront at the sink. He's not classically handsome, but all the parts come together for an appealing whole. He has thinning hair, but his nice skin makes up for that. He's five feet, ten inches tall, which means I fit comfortably under his arm. He's trim, has excellent posture, and the man knows how to dress.

He also knows how to stand his ground. The upcoming discussion I've planned could go all kinds of ways. He might be all in on moving or… not.

Turning from the sink, he takes off his glasses. "I think I made it worse."

Oh, things are going to get worse.

Out loud I say, "Go change and let's eat. There's something I want to discuss. Oh, and I'm sorry about dinner. We're having soup. I forgot to thaw the chicken."

Campbell looks surprised. "You forgot?" He sees my raised eyebrows and heads for the bedroom without another word.

After our improvised dinner, I move his plate and set down the most recent photo of Max, fifteen months. In it, he has one hand on a coffee table for support. In his other hand, he's clutching a stuffed dolphin, courtesy of *moi*. His grin says he finds the world hilarious.

Campbell smiles. "Definitely Gerber Baby material."

"Isn't he adorable? Don't you want to see that face in person more than you do?"

"Well, sure, but that's why we go visit all the time. Like six times since he was born." He sounds wary.

"It's not enough. We're going to miss important milestones, like him throwing a ball, learning to read, losing a tooth, riding his bike without training wheels."

"You can't be suggesting… well, this is… are you saying…" When Campbell gets what we call befuffled, he loses the ability to finish a sentence.

"I want to know him, *really* know him. As an every-single-day part of his life." These words are only partly true. I'm saying we need to know Max. The truth is I want Max to know me.

"I've summed up my thinking on this chart," I tell him, placing a piece of paper on the table.

Colorado	Ohio
Max	No Max

Campbell glances at the paper but is not amused at my joke. "But Jay hasn't lived near us for years. That doesn't bother you."

"I've been thinking about that. We had all of Jay's grow-ing-up years to spend with him, to be close, to form a tight bond. That bond will always be there, no matter how far apart we live. But Max? If we aren't close and make a strong connec-tion now, it'll never happen. I don't want that. Do you?"

"Of course not, but what are you saying? Move there? Where did this come from? Besides, it sounds like you've made up your mind already, which I don't appreciate. What happened to discussing it and making a decision together?"

I've made a tactical error. Now, instead of focusing on whether or not to move, Campbell is going to make this about my methods and manner. In other words, about me.

I'm an idiot.

I mentally give myself three lashes and backtrack. "We are discussing it, right now. I mean, are you willing to consider a move? It's beautiful out there. I bet we'd love it." But my diversionary maneuvers are too little, too late. Round one to Campbell.

My husband pushes back his chair. Stands and glares. "I've got PTA. You need to cool your jets. We've never been grandparents before, and we'll find the rhythm of it. There's a middle way."

Campbell has a favorite expression, a verbal test to sort

his priorities and figure out where to put his mental energy. He asks himself, "Do I want to die on that hill?" He's right. You have to pick your battles if you want to win the war.

I'm willing to die on the Max hill.

to do list

- Wear Campbell down
- Order maps from AAA
- Wear Campbell down
- Wear Campbell down
-
-
-
-
-
-
-
-

CHAPTER FIVE

Winter/Spring

Siege

Campbell and I have reversed roles.

Normally in our relationship, I'm the clear-eyed manager, and he's the impulsive risk-taker. He pushes. I resist. It works, so that even when we take it to a battle royal, a bloody compromise emerges.

I'm the pusher this time; he's the pushee. *Or the pushover.* I picture Campbell toppling as I apply steady pressure. My first domino! Visualization, they call it. I will break bricks with my mind. Bend spoons. Move mountains. Move *us* to the mountains.

He's a formidable foe, and I don't help my cause by agreeing with most of his arguments.

"You're right. You've put together a great staff, but…"

"Yes, a cross-country move will cost around $10,000, but…"

"We did just remodel the bathroom, but…"

"I am up for a raise, but…"

"Your parents are getting older, but…"

In February I celebrate my sixty-second birthday. Inside, I feel about forty-five. Outside? I study myself in the full length mirror in our bedroom, trying for objectivity. I went gray early, and after one disastrous hair coloring incident, I decided to let nature take its course. I keep my hair short, so I can manage it myself. All I need is a good cut.

I continue my inventory. Thick, gray hair. Blue eyes. Nice skin, if you can look past the wrinkles around my mouth, and more neck than one person should possess. I throw my shoulders back, conscious that gravity is trying to win the war against my posture. I have regular features, decent legs, and bad feet. I work hard to keep my weight down, but it takes constant vigilance. I like cookies and ice cream as much as the next person, and I'll treat myself from time to time, but I try to focus on fruits, vegetables, and protein.

Campbell tells me I'm pretty, but I think that's an adjective for a younger woman. I don't want to be *handsome,* that deadly compliment. Maybe I'm … striking? Attractive for my age? Well preserved? I give up and get dressed. Cover up the stretch marks, hike up the breasts that want to visit my waist, and get on with life. Max will love me, regardless.

We push through the dreary weeks of a Midwestern winter. Gloomy days. Dirty snow. Icy roads. I can't help but count the days until spring break. We go to Denver, where the sun is shining, the air is dry, and Max, like a consummate salesman, keeps lobbing incentives our way: hugs, kisses, snuggles!

Back home, we resume our Max-less life. Luckily, I have our Skype sessions to look forward to. Jay holds Max up to the camera as Campbell and I coo like pigeons.

One evening during our debrief, as we're sharing the triumphs and tragedies of the day, Campbell cracks. "If we did move, how could we get jobs there as good as what we have here?"

As my mother used to say: *It's all over but the shouting.*

I go to my desk, fish out two stapled pages, and drop them in his lap. "With the updates I've made to your résumé, you could probably notch it up and interview for superintendent positions."

Campbell doesn't want to be a superintendent. He could be. He has his doctorate and superintendent's license, but he prefers the life of a principal. Running a building. Managing a staff. Helping kids. King of his kingdom.

"You updated my résumé? Rook, you are…" He can't think of an appropriate word so I supply some.

"Thoughtful? Helpful?"

He shakes his head. "I think 'ballsy' is the word I'm looking for."

Despite this dig, he agrees to start job hunting. *Another domino!* Our lives become a slog of filling out applications, haunting websites, phoning leads. We persevere even though we have one little problem. I've always made more money than Campbell, which has been fine with him. But duplicating my salary and benefits, at sixty-two?

We have serious meetings with Bob Hale, our financial guy. We construct various scenarios, consider actuarial tables, talk about what we'd like to leave Jay as an inheritance, build spreadsheets, and generally get confused and anxious. I mention retirement, but Bob is not a fan.

"One of you or the other, maybe. But not both, not this young."

Campbell puts the kibosh on his retirement. "No way. I like what I do. You retire if you want, but I'm not ready. Not negotiable."

What was I thinking?

In May, we make a last effort: flying to Denver so that Campbell can take an interview, and I can look at houses. After a day of traipsing around with a real estate agent, I'm taking a break in a Starbucks, nursing an Earl Grey tea, and working up an austerity budget, when my cell phone rings.

"Hello, dear wife, this is your future calling." Campbell is delighted with himself. He's the new principal of a K-5 school in the foothills outside Denver. That night, over a celebratory dinner at Jay and Carly's, Campbell thrills me when he says, "If we're moving to Colorado, let's not buy a house down here in Denver, where we're just looking west towards the mountains, but let's live *in* them."

The next day, we revisit a house I like in Grant Falls, which puts us 8,000 feet above sea level. Campbell would be thirty minutes from work, and we'd be twenty minutes from the center of our universe: Max. We cross our fingers and make an offer. They counter. We counter back. They accept.

We fly back to Ohio in shock. "I guess we're doing this," Campbell tells me, opening his bag of airline peanuts. "We've crossed the Rubicon, although in our case, it's the Mississippi."

I'm too stunned to answer.

I hand in my resignation, which is a hard day. I've made it

in the tough, testosterone-infused world of IT, and giving it up causes a pang. Even if it's just temporary. I bury these thoughts under the demands of my new position: Move Director. My last day at the bank comes quickly. I collect a beautiful Mont Blanc pen set and walk out on a thirty-eight-year career.

Our friends think we're nuts, uprooting ourselves. We've heard everything: *You're moving halfway across the country? You're moving without a job? What if Jay and Carly move to California? Won't you hate living in a small town? Do you ski? It snows a TON there. Are you going to babysit every day?*

Here's the thing: I don't ski. I've never lived in the mountains. I'm unsure about living in a small town. I'm worried I may never replace my salary and benefits.

Campbell will be OK. He's a great principal, and the kids, teachers, and parents of Elk Meadow Elementary will love him.

Everyone is counting on me, and I can handle that. Give me an objective, and I'll make it happen. The perfect move, the perfect new home, the perfect new job, the perfect grandmother.

NOTE TO SELF
Cross naysaying "friends" off Christmas card list.

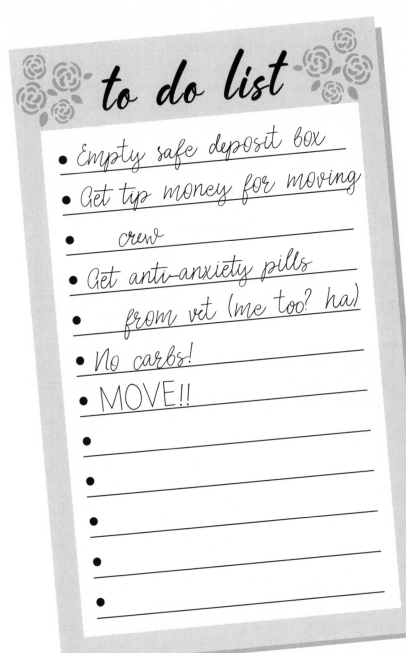

to do list

- Empty safe deposit box
- Get tip money for moving
- crew
- Get anti-anxiety pills
- from vet (me too? ha)
- No carbs!
- MOVE!!

CHAPTER SIX

June

Convoy

C ampbell, the wagon master, leads our two-car cara-van across the country.

"Why's he in front?" I ask Sammie, scrunched in her travel crate on the passenger seat, ears back. "I ordered the maps, planned the route, and packed the snacks."

Sammie looks worried. Does she need a break? I'm not adept at reading faces—dog or human. I'm not good at remembering them either. Campbell has that talent, thank God. We joke he could be a private eye; he's so skilled at absorbing his surroundings. He's learned to lean in and whisper, "That's the man who did our landscaping," or "She's the receptionist in the vet's office." I even laugh when he makes fun of me. "That's your sister-in-law," or "He lives next door."

My affliction has created embarrassing moments, the worst

being at my cousin Tom's funeral. I approached a man standing near the casket and made a calculated guess that it was Tom's brother, my cousin, Harris. Touching him on the sleeve, I said, "I'm so sorry about Tom. I'm sure you have many wonderful memories of growing up together."

The man smiled politely. "Ma'am, I do have wonderful childhood memories, but I grew up in Pennsylvania with two sisters. I'm the funeral director."

"He looks a bit like Harris, doesn't he?" I asked Campbell later near the guest book.

He was putting in overtime, feeding me the names and relationships of people who came up, arms open for a hug, dredging up old stories. My cousin Janet repeats a time-worn story. "Rook, remember when we had that sleepover when we were kids? You told everybody to go to sleep at eleven o'clock. What a little drill sergeant you were!"

Haha, Cousin Janet. Yes, I'm opinionated, but like my favorite mug says, "I'm Not Bossy, I Just Have Better Ideas."

I hope this move is one of those better ideas. I glance at the map I've spread on the console.

"Sammie? Would you like to stop? Think we could find a Whole Foods?"

I pick up the cell phone I've tucked in the cup holder and call Campbell.

"How about a break? Sammie needs to pee, and so do I." He agrees and ten minutes later takes an exit and parks at a McDonald's. Not what I'd have picked, but at least you know what you're getting. *Fried with a side of fried*, says my internal food police. Knowing I won't leave Sammie in a closed car even for ten minutes, my husband waves at me and goes in.

I glance at my new watch, an anniversary present from Campbell. It's beautiful and elegant, and I love it. We'd gone out to dinner to celebrate thirty-nine years together, and he surprised me with a small, artfully wrapped box after dessert. I was thrilled with the stylish and graceful watch inside. "This is gorgeous. Thank you! Oh, I need to set it. It's—" Then I saw his grin and understood. He'd set the watch to the Mountain Time Zone. Colorado time. Our new home. I'd presented him with a handsome leather portfolio to use at his new job, but the watch? And the gesture? Like the ad says: *Priceless*.

I can feel the heat on my skin as I walk Sammie around the burnt grass next to the parking lot. It must be ninety degrees. The sun is soaking the asphalt and reheating a pile of fries dumped in the mulch, which captures Sammie's attention. Campbell exits the McDonald's, jumping out of the way of an SUV accelerating away from the pick-up window.

"Asshole," he yells. He hands me an iced tea and slurps his smoothie.

"Now what would the Elk Meadow parents think, hearing their new principal talking like that? Is that your mascot? The Elks? Maybe you're the Mountain Goats? The Marmots? The Weasels?"

Campbell smiles. "The Eagles. The Screaming Eagles. How are you doing? How much longer until we stop for the night? A Marriott maybe?" There's hope in his voice.

"We've got about one hundred miles. Sorry, not a Marriott, but it takes dogs. I'm doing OK. I've certainly developed a new respect for long-haul truckers."

I don't share that I'm constipated, stiff from holding the ten-and-two-o'clock position on the wheel, and desperate for some validation that this move was a good idea.

Campbell looks at Sammie, who has discovered a morsel of hamburger bun in the dirt. "You know how the pioneers would cast off possessions to lighten their wagons? I have a nomination for the next discard." He waggles his eyebrows at me, which I ignore. He talks trash about Sammie all the time, but I know the truth. He takes her out first thing in the morning, despite the weather. He holds her while I clip her toenails, blowing into her neck while she swoons with delight. I love Sammie, and he loves me, so Sammie gets a pass.

Campbell finishes his smoothie, tosses the cup in the trash, and turns to ponder the endless Kansas prairie, rolling away uninhibited toward... what? Nebraska? South Dakota? As a kid, I had a wooden puzzle map of the United States, each state a brightly colored piece, its capital city marked with a star. What's north of Kansas? The landscape suggests there's nothing except cornfields until you hit Canada.

He gestures toward the wide-open spaces. "Dorothy wanted to get back to this?"

"Not this. Auntie Em and Uncle Henry. To family."

He grunts. Then surprises me by squeezing his eyes shut, shuffling his sandaled heels together and intoning, "There's no place like Colorado. There's no place like Colorado." He opens one eye and sighs. "Well, that didn't work. Guess we'll have to drive."

We buckle in, Sammie curls into a ball inside her crate, and I steel myself to grind out another two hours. Campbell's got me thinking about the *Wizard of Oz*. If I were standing before the Wizard, what would I ask for? What would Campbell ask for?

Like most long-married couples, we've developed theories and opinions about each other that hold a kernel of truth, but which we exaggerate for dramatic effect. Thus, the accepted wisdom is that I am competent, coolheaded, and a bit hard-hearted, while Campbell is warm, but forgetful, like the absent-minded professor.

I snicker and tell Sammie, "Here's how it would go, Sam. I'd ask the Wizard to give him a brain…"

Signaling her agreement, my dog turns in her crate and puts a paw through the bars.

"… and he'd request that I get a heart."

to do list

- Call plumber
- Find Cs math curriculum
- bks
- ID smell: dead bird in
- chimney? Ick.
- Take moving boxes to
- recycle
- Sch babysitting dates for
- Max
- f/u on job leads
- Find local Weight Watchers
- mtg b/f it's too late!

CHAPTER SEVEN

July

Adjusting

C ampbell turns over in bed, dragging the top sheet with him.

I sleep with the covers tucked in all around me and up to my neck, and he's ruined my cocoon. I've asked him dozens of times, nicely, to turn over without exposing me to the cool night air. His response?

"Goddamn it, Rook. I'm asleep. You can't expect me to be thinking about you when I turn over, IN MY SLEEP."

I concede his point, but my resentment lingers as I rearrange my nest, execute a perfect swivel maneuver, and look at the clock—4:38 a.m. Just enough sleep to make it through the coming day but not enough to enjoy it. I'll spend the next ninety minutes obsessing about the house, the move, and my endless "To Do" list.

The excitement of leaving the Midwest and starting life in the mountains has faded. Campbell is focused solely on his new job. His predecessor had serious hoarding tendencies. When Campbell unlocked the door of his office, he found every table and chair stacked with paper, books, notices, flyers, and assorted paraphernalia, not to mention every file drawer filled. I can't get his attention right now.

That leaves me to fight the good fight as I unpack, figure out how stuff works, and give myself pep talks. I miss the routine of my job and the casual camaraderie. But I can't tell anyone that, except Sammie.

I replay the conversation from yesterday's debrief. Campbell had come home from work, changed, and we'd settled on the matching chairs in the family room.

"Who wants to go first?" Campbell begins. "You? No? OK, I'll go. I had a pretty good day. I met several of my teachers, who came in to organize their classrooms and put up new bulletin board displays. I threw out half a dumpster's worth of crap from my office. My second grade teachers want to attend a reading conference in Denver, and I said yes. Oh yeah, the PTA president asked if I'd sit in the dunk tank at the PTA carnival in September."

"Principal McFadden in a bathing suit? I'd pay to see that."

"Ah… number one, I'd wear shorts and a T-shirt. Number two, it's not happening." Campbell stops and wrinkles his nose. "There's that smell again. Did you figure it out?"

"No, I was busy doing a bunch of other stuff. Like looking for your math books, which I have for you, by the way. I had to open five boxes to find them."

"I appreciate it. But that smell. I think you should call a

chimney sweep, or maybe an exterminator? Can you make it a priority?"

Sure, Campbell. I'll make it a priority, along with the hundred other things you want done.

Moving is the pits. The mountain house has given us several shocks, most notably the mysterious orange stain on the carpet in the office. It's slowly revealing its true nature: a leaky kitchen faucet, a garage door that makes a high-pitched squeal, a sticky back door.

I don't mind getting things fixed. I just want it to be straightforward. Take the leaky faucet. Solution? Call a plumber. However, one would have to know the number of a plumber to be able to do that. If you're new to the area, you have to ask your neighbor, which presumes you have met your neighbor or gone over to your neighbor's home to introduce yourself so that you could ask them for a recommendation. Result? The faucet drips, and you stew, and you want to smack your husband when he asks, "Did you call a plumber?"

Sammie rustles in her crate. She seems to like the mountains, although I have to watch her like a hawk because the hawks are watching her, well, like hawks. She's the perfect snack for many of the predators around here, so she gets no unsupervised time outside.

We all have our crosses to bear. Principal McFadden might have to give up his dignity at the PTA carnival. I have to whip this house into shape and find a job. Sammie has to walk on a leash.

It just takes time.

A year from now it'll all be running smoothly. I remind myself to think about the good stuff: the ponderosa pines, the elk herds who wander through the neighborhood, and most importantly, Max's smile.

I'll eventually beat the house into submission. I'm not so sure about finding a new job. I'm doing my part. I'm following every dictate of a successful job search. I get up like I'm going to work. I dress like I'm going to work. I sit in my home office and click away at my keyboard. Short coffee breaks. Thirty minutes for lunch. It's exactly like being at work, except I'm not at work.

I can't explain it. I'm qualified, experienced, and my résumé is dripping with accomplishments. This should be a slam-dunk. My technical relevance is draining away, along with my confidence.

I am, however, an excellent babysitter. Conscientious, alert, and besotted with my charge. I watch Max one day a week, an oasis in my job-hunting desert. I smile, remembering our last time together. When I heard Max grumbling in his crib, I listened at the door, then pushed it open a few inches. I expected to see him prone, mid-nap, but he's standing at the end of the crib, peering at me in the half-light. We giggle. Sammie is spinning at my feet, eager to lick Max. They've become close. Max likes her water dish, and she's interested in his diaper pail.

I go to Max and kiss the top of his head. He leans into me, a sweet weight. I begin what has become our routine, the verbal handshake known only to members of the Gram & Max Club.

"Who's my best boy?" His breath is like a feather tickling my neck.

"Ax," he says. I squeeze him tighter.

"Who loves Max to the max?"

He hesitates, then whispers in my ear, "Gam." I close my eyes and treasure this exchange.

Yes, I'm unemployed. I've traded project management for toddler management. I'm using my organizational skills to arrange the kitchen cabinets. But… I feel… contented. After a lifetime of fighting my way into the boys' club, I find myself in the kitchen and nursery, and I'm shocked to admit:

I like it.

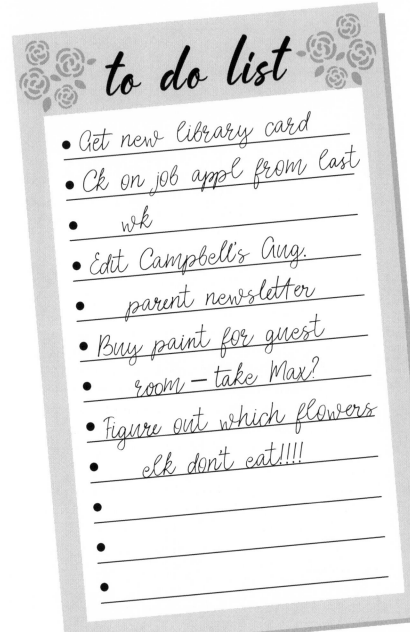

to do list

- Get new library card
- Ck on job appl from last
-    wk
- Edit Campbell's Aug.
-    parent newsletter
- Buy paint for guest
-    room — take Max?
- Figure out which flowers
-    elk don't eat!!!!
-
-
-

CHAPTER EIGHT

July

Recess

Today is my playdate with Max.

It's the highlight of my week. On my planner, I've printed "Babysitting," but that's a misnomer. For one thing, Max is no baby, but a twenty-one-month-old flash of lightning. I won't sit either, but crawl, squat, hide, crouch, bend, and chase one determined toddler. I haven't had this much fun in years.

Driving down from Grant Falls, I chat with my inner child.

Adult Me: "How does Play-Doh sound today?"

Inner Child: "Whee."

Adult Me: "We could do the hokey pokey and turn ourselves about."

Inner Child: "Whee."

Adult Me: "Do you ever say no to anything?"

Inner Child: "Whee."

After Carly leaves for work, Max and I settle in an armchair with a sizeable stack of picture books. I point to animals and grunt, cackle, neigh, and oink my way through the barnyard menagerie. I'm especially proud of my chicken. Max does a mean "Baa" and "Moo." Finally, we top it off with several choruses of "Old McDonald."

"Let's walk up to the playground." I put Max in his stroller, and we set off, with me commenting on whatever presents itself. A neighbor walking her dog. "Woof." The mailman. A squirrel. A leaf. A fireman, straight out of central casting, working on a nearby hydrant. The world moves at a different speed when I'm with Max. It unfolds, full of beautiful illustrations, like the picture books we read earlier, each page promising delight.

At the playground, Max wants to drive the life-size wooden tractor and play in the sandbox. I watch for small discoveries to point out to him: a cat trotting across a corner of the park, a helicopter buzzing overhead, a rose bush, an anthill. We find an empty water bottle and carry it to the trashcan. I crouch down and look at the play equipment from his perspective. It's huge. Equivalent to my trying to climb a house. Kids are amazing and brave—what they learn and master in just a few months. I resolve to master my environment with less carping. I give Max a hug for teaching his Gram a life lesson and relish his arms around my neck.

Back home, we play with blocks, pretend to be lions, and have, perhaps, too many crackers for Carly's liking. After I put him down to nap, I work on my laptop, checking job sites, submitting applications, and nursing my frustration.

What's wrong with these people? Here I am—an outstanding

potential employee—and I might as well be invisible. If I had known how hard… I wish… I stop this train of thought right away. Like my mother said: *If wishes were horses, then beggars would ride.*

Scratch the wishing. "It'll happen. I'll make it happen. Sons of bitches."

I hear Max fussing after an hour and throw open his bedroom door. "Ta-da!"

"Gam!"

I kneel on the floor and wiggle my fingers through the slats of his crib. Pulling back a little, I'm hit with an odor that makes my eyes water. The boy I put down smelled like powder and crackers.

"Do you have a poopy diaper?"

He shakes his head. "Nooo." An outrageous fib.

"How was your nap?"

"Fire truck."

I laugh at this adorable non-sequitur. This is exactly why we moved: to witness his joy in neighborhood dogs and pine-cones. Read "The Bad Bunny" fifteen times in a row. Wipe and powder his behind. Watch him discover his gifts.

I dance my fingers on the mattress, and Max walks his over for an introduction. We wave and bow and hop away and end the *pas de deux* with our fingers entwined. I breathe a prayer that it will always be so. My perfect boy.

"Let's change your diaper."

"Nooo."

I march a stuffed bear along the top rail of the crib. Mr. Bear swoops down to Max's backside and sniffs. Recoils. "Oh no," he squeaks, "Max needs a new diaper."

Max giggles. "Udder bear," he commands.

I search through his pile of stuffed animals, tossing aside a giraffe, a cat, and a dozen other candidates before finding Udder Bear. He repeats the inspection of Max's bottom and confirms the diagnosis by fainting.

"Max, you want to see a trick?" I position the smaller bear on the top bar and flip him, and he performs an astonishing triple summersault before landing on his face. Max demands an encore before consenting to a diaper change. He really is the perfect child.

Changing Max turns into changing every single thing he's wearing. We pick out a new outfit and I put his dirty ones in the laundry room to soak.

"Are you hungry?"

"Malk. Bar. Blupberries."

"OK, malk," I repeat without thinking. "I mean milk. Some cut-up banana. Then what shall we do? Would you like to go for a ride with Gram? We could run a couple of errands."

Max heads for his toy cars, and while I prepare his snack, he lines them up in the family room.

"Rrrmmm," he shouts, spinning them into the wall and under the couch. He loads his plastic wheelbarrow with vehicles and darts around the room, hiding them behind lamps and under cushions. In this game he's invented, he's large and in charge.

My parenting philosophy is simple: If you can say yes, say yes. I won't let Max cross the street by himself or eat an entire box of cookies, but build a fort in the living room? Wear his shorts on his head? Ride the mechanical pony at the grocery store? Yes, yes, and yes.

The world will take the wind out of his sails soon enough.

to do list

- Find new vet
- Find new church
- Find new job
- Find new dry cleaner
- Find new attitude
-
-
-
-
-
-
-

CHAPTER NINE

July

Errands

T he straps of Max's car seat twist and warp under my novice fingers.

"AARRGH!" My shout, halfway between pirate and growly bear, delights my grandson.

"Arrrr," he imitates.

Three days after arriving in Colorado, Campbell and I went out and bought two of the best child car seats we could find, one for each of our cars. Back at our new home, I washed out cupboards in the kitchen while Campbell installed the seats, a steady stream of curses floating in from the garage.

"You son of a… get in there, you miserable—ouch! Goddamn it… shit!"

Thank God for Jay. He gave us an in-person tutorial, walking us through how to loosen the straps, then buckle them, double-checking the position of the top set, and finally, pulling them just tight enough to be effective but loose enough so Max could breathe. I watched, but it reminded me of a flight attendant demonstrating how to fasten and unfasten a lap belt, holding one over her head like we'd all just crawled out from under a rock. *Please!* If you didn't know how to operate a seat belt, you were *dumb as a candy frog,* as Mom used to say.

"You know what, Max? I've never done this. It's always been your mom or dad or granddad, but I can do this. How hard can it be?"

Turns out it's hard. Max wiggles and squirms, compounding my poor performance. I feel a split second of affection for the good old days when kids bounced around the back seat unrestrained.

"Are you in there right?"

His seat faces the rear, so I'm bent awkwardly across him, inches from his face. I take advantage of our proximity to give him a kiss.

"Love you."

I listen for the clicks that signal success, test the play in the straps, and straighten the sippy cup of water snug in its very own cup holder. The king on his throne.

Running errands with a toddler is crazy. We should stay home and bake cookies or play with his Noah's Ark set.

"Are you ready, Max? Let's get out and see the sights."

My real motivation is on the passenger seat: my "To Do" list, emitting a siren's call. Metro Denver is a retail mecca compared to Grant Falls. I've made the drive down here, and I'm not about to let the opportunity go to waste, even if it means fighting Max in and out of his car seat multiple times.

At Sherwin Williams, Max plays with color sample cards while I buy two cans of paint and have them shaken up. He's gravitated to the reds so I give him six cards, which he shuffles and spills and picks up and arranges. I'm buying paint for the guest room, currently a god-awful green. We've picked a color, Chalk. Why Chalk is better than Foam, Frost, or Artic Ice, I can't say. They are all, however, superior to Hideous Green.

The fanciful names are a hoot. Complementing my skill deficiency in reading and remembering faces is a similar deficiency in differentiating shades and tones of color. I even object to the acronym for the colors in the rainbow: ROY G. BIV. I'd jettison Indigo and Violet and go with Purple. ROY G. BP.

I open the rear hatch of my Ford Escape, only to find the storage compartment full of plastic boxes.

"Campbell, you…" I'm about to disparage my husband when I see Max watching me. *Little pitchers have big ears.* I bite back my expletive, leaving it unspoken but not unthought. It's Campbell's school stuff. He treats cars like filing cabinets on wheels, which has caused any number of arguments.

The boxes are two deep and two high, and there's no floor space. I try lifting one, but it's heavy, full of books and binders. Moving them is not an option. I put the paint on top of the box nearest the cargo door, on the opposite side of the car from Max. I don't want to spoil his already limited view, and I certainly don't want them falling over on him. I find a small travel blanket snaked around the boxes and wrench it free. Tuck it around the cans to keep them stable. I'm about to close the hatch when inspired, I crouch and hide my face behind the cans.

"Where's Max?" I call in the standard singsong, before

popping out. Max chuckles, and I chalk one up for the golden oldies.

The second stop is an outdoor nursery. I put my impressive command of colors to work for Max's edification, pointing out yellow flowers, red flowers, orange flowers. Max, strapped in a cart, spots a pond.

"Wadder," he announces, happy to contribute to the conversation.

I push him over to the pond, and we're rewarded. Orange koi fish drift in the currents while green water lilies dot the surface. Ceramic frogs perch on the sides. Max wants to touch a fish, but we compromise on waving to them. I get him down from the cart and we trail our fingers through the water. We leave wetter than we arrived.

"Max, which do you like better? The ficus or the schefflera?"

He's busy telling me a long story that involves fish and frogs and water, and he can't be bothered. I select the ficus. It takes fifteen minutes to check out and get the monster plant wheeled to the car. It's too tall for the rear storage compartment, now full of boxes and paint, so I ask the garden center staff to put it on the floor in the back seat.

I loosen the straps on Max's seat, then hoist him in. As I engage the buckles, I listen for the clicks while simultaneously testing that the plant is out of his reach. Otherwise, I'll arrive home with a new species: *Ficus denudus*.

As I pull back, I can't resist his neck. I puff out my cheeks and blow into it, making that rude farting sound beloved by all boys and most men.

"Heeheehee. Again."

When I slide behind the wheel, the ficus touches the back

of my head. I adjust the driver's seat forward and into its full upright setting. It's cramped and awkward, "But worth it," I tell Max, "because we can cross two items off our list. Plus we had fun at the paint store and playing in the water. Right?"

Max's response is "Mmmmwadderuuhh," which I decide is yes.

As I head for home, I congratulate myself on my competency as a grandmother/babysitter/errand-runner. My seat belt is uncomfortable, but I ignore that. A stray thought tickles my brain, *Did I tighten Max's belt?* I replay the sequence: loosen, buckle two times, click two times, position, tighten. *Of course I did.*

"Max, want to hear some music?"

An exit sign flashes by and I suck in my breath. "That can't be right. Wait a minute."

One advantage to finding your way around Denver and its environs is the mountains are always west. They're big, you can't miss them, and they're always west. The trouble is that they're now in my rearview mirror, which means.... "I'm going east, Max. How the hell…?"

The next exit isn't for three miles, and when I take it, I have to go another half mile before finding a strip mall so that I can turn around. My blood pressure edges up. My error has cost us fifteen minutes, and it's another ten before I settle down. *No harm done,* I soothe myself. *You're on the right track now. Relax.*

Max is talking nonstop while I enjoy the ride. Is there a more beautiful state than Colorado? No humidity, no bugs, astonishing skies, constant sunshine, and the *pièce de résistance*: the Rocky Mountains. The only hiccup is my failure to find a job.

I'm surprised and embarrassed at this state of affairs. I'm

used to planning and arranging my life to get the outcome I want. A leads to B, which leads to C, connect the dots, and *voilà*. Except this time the dots aren't connecting.

"My résumé is solid, Max. I interview well. I've applied for dozens of jobs. What gives, huh? Am I too old?"

Max doesn't have an opinion on my job search and has stopped chattering.

"Hey, buddy-boy, what's the matter?" I try a quick look but my seat position is costing me my usual maneuverability, plus he's obscured by his car seat. "You OK? Did you drop your water?"

"Wadder not working." Max sounds aggrieved. His sippy cup must have malfunctioned.

"Sorry, love, but I can't fix it now. I'll fix it when we get to your house."

Wadder not working. Ha. Good one. Like my job search. Job search not working.

I refocus on my driving. It starts to sprinkle, so I turn on the intermittent wipers. I slow down and take the entrance ramp that will merge me onto the interstate. I hate this style of interchange, and they're common in Denver. The design forces you to speed up and merge at the same place that someone else wants to slow down and exit, both on the same side of the highway. *Crisscross, applesauce.* My head is spinning like the girl in *The Exorcist* as I try to look in four directions at once.

I accelerate off the ramp, glance in my rearview mirror, hit the turn signal, and move left.

Home free.

to do list

- Please God Help
- Please God
- Please
-
-
-
-
-
-
-
-
-

CHAPTER TEN

July

Frenzy

The world explodes.

Stabs of sound, blotches of color, and the physical sensation of being inside a blender when someone hits the ON switch assault me.

First? A huge noise—equal parts screech, crash, and squeal—fills the space around me. It swells and rolls, amplified by blaring car horns and shrieking tires.

The Escape is pushed violently to the right, but some unknown barrier shoves us away as if two magnetic forces are repelling each other. The car rocks, tilts, trembles. I hear screams, but whether it's me, Max, or both of us, I don't know.

The air inside the car feels compressed. Something large blasts by my ear and smashes into the windshield. Dirt clouds swirl in slow-motion, an effect I've only seen in movies. I catch glimpses of sky, concrete, sky. Something viscous slaps me in the face, and I instinctively close my eyes.

I'm pushed against my seat belt with stunning force. I shout out my surprise and protest and fear as the car rolls and rolls and slams to a stop.

The screaming now comes only from Max. Kids have different cries. One for tired. One for frightened. One for hungry. This one is for pure terror. It cuts through my confusion.

The car is upside down. I hang suspended in my harness, blinking and choking on the dirty air.

Oh my God.

My heart thumps. We're helpless. We've survived whatever just happened only to be crushed by a truck barreling at us right this second. I have to get Max out.

"Max," I shout.

I struggle with my belt, but my weight has it locked tight. I twist to see the back seat, but objects aren't where I expect. Up is down. Metal is crumpled and distorted. I see the edge of Max's car seat. The car reeks of paint.

"Max? Max! I'm coming. Please, please, speak to Gram. Are you OK?"

Begging.

Silence.

"Max?"

Hysteria.

Get a grip, Rook.

Silence.

The awful sound of silence.

I strain to remember strapping Max in, pulling the belts tight, positioning them in the right place.

He's safe. He's OK. He's safe. He's OK. He's safe…

Pounding.

I turn and stare at a man who appears to be standing on his head. He moves his mouth and waves his arms.

"Stay… police… way."

I concentrate. The car sits in grass.

"Mr.? Mr.? Grandson. In back. Help. My grandson."

I shake, chilled, my breath a series of ragged gulps.

The noise outside wells up, a deafening mix of sirens and shouts and engines.

The seat belt refuses to open. Inside the car, inside the silence, a high-pitched keening.

Like a bug pinned to a board, my only view is directly in front of me: the windshield, cracked and crazed.

My neck hurts. My chest hurts. I can't move, and I can't stop wailing, so I do the only other thing I can think of. Pray. *Father, protect us. Merciful God, help us. Lord, comfort Max.* When the helmeted fireman looks in at me, I'm in a land of unreason, horror, and fear.

Voices near my window. "Stabilize…. hot zone… captain… tool… airbag…"

Other voices by the back doors. "Child… jacks… trauma…"

I hear sirens, shouts, undecipherable bursts from radios.

Max's door is wrenched open and there are clicks, mumbling, some questions I can't follow, and the voices ebb.

After an eternity, two firemen cut my belt and I'm lowered down and out of the car.

"Ma'am, can you talk to me? What's your name?"

I stand, wobbling. The only name I can think of is "Gam."

"What's your age?"

That I know. "Sixty-two."

"Was anybody else in the car with you?"

I moan Max's name over and over. "Maxmaxmax." A mantra. An incantation.

"Max is your—"

"Grandson," I cut him off. "Where? Want…"

"We have him. We're taking him to Children's. Anyone else?"

"Just Max." I use my boss voice but we all can hear the tremor in it. "Where is he? How is he? I need to see him."

"They've already left with him. Sorry, but due to a hospital diversion, we'll be taking you to a different facility."

This makes no sense, and I want to scream.

"Let's see about you, OK?"

"No. Not me. I'm OK. I have to be with—can I go?"

"So you're refusing medical assistance?"

Why can't I make this nice first responder understand? I want Max. I nod, and he leads me away from the totaled Escape to stand next to a highway patrol car. I try to form sensible impressions, but my eyes have been replaced with kaleidoscopes. Everywhere I look I see intensely colored fragments duplicating, melding, twirling. They join and separate in a dizzying effect—light bars on top of police cars, brake lights, strobes, raindrops, pulsing flashes on ambulances. I close my eyes to shut it out, but what I see then, eyes squeezed shut, is a windshield, cracked and crazed.

Broken. It's all broken.

I don't feel well. There's no moisture in my mouth and my bones are dissolving, passing through some gel-like stage on their way to liquid.

I open my eyes. Try again. This time I see, like a camera pulling back, a panoramic view of the disaster. Police cars from every jurisdiction—state, county, city—stacked up along the roadway. I count but lose track. Five? Six? More pull up.

A fire truck sits across the highway, and firemen drag hoses and carry equipment around as part of a well-choreographed production. A huge rescue truck and three ambulances glitter in the raindrops. A second fire truck arrives.

Traffic is at a complete stop. I put a hand to my face. I'm splattered with paint. I notice a second car, crushed and also upside down, in the median. Two separate crews of medics kneel on the ground. *The idiot who hit me.*

I try to reconstruct the moments before the crash. *I checked my mirror, the lane was clear, I moved over, I got hit.* I repeat the sequence, memorizing it. Some fool on their phone. A drunk.

Call Campbell. He'll come, and we can go to where Max is.

I command myself to do this, but my hands hang limp, useless. I move my head to the right, left, and down, looking for my purse and my phone. I feel peculiar. Streaks of light pulse in my peripheral vision. An ache is forming behind my forehead. I spread my feet farther apart to keep my balance.

What's wrong with my eyes? Now everything is retreating, rushing away like looking through the wrong end of a telescope.

I see a tiny image of a car wreck, a sepia-tone postcard. Red fire trucks and yellow ambulances appear grey. No sound. No sirens. No shouting. I don't feel anything on my skin. No breeze. No rain.

I look down and notice the solid white line marking the side of the highway. I stare, swaying, fixated. Something about the line is important. Lines. Boundaries. Borders.

"Ma'am? Are you all right?" A young trooper stands in front of me. He puts out a hand to steady me, then jogs off. "Let me get the EMTs."

His instincts are good. I'm seconds away from keeling over. Before I do, I have to call...? *Concentrate!* Who do I have to call? *Or is it, "Whom do I have to call?"*

I force myself to focus. Oh, yes. I need to call Campbell and tell him that the life we moved across the country to build is shattered.

I have to call Jay and tell him that his conscientious, responsible mother has just hurt his son in some unknown but devastating way.

I have to call Carly and tell her that her mother-in-law cannot be trusted.

I notice the line again; the meaning now clear. It marks a separation, a division: life before today, and life after.

Two medics arrive. "Ma'am? Is there pain? Where's your pain? Can you describe your pain?" I look at these professionals, puzzled. *Isn't it obvious? There's pain, and it's indescribable.*

I fold to the ground, weighted by despair.

I want to be with Max. Wherever he is.

Six shoes point toward me in a loose semi-circle. My stomach heaves, the shoes step away, hands reach.

Crying, gagging, more abject and alone than I've ever been in my life, I struggle to my hands and knees, and head bowed, retch until there's nothing left.

to do list

- must see Max
- get police report
- eat
-
-
-
-
-
-
-
-

CHAPTER ELEVEN

July

Hell

My mind is on a continuous loop.

Max. Accident. Hospital. Police. Max. Accident. Hospital. Police. Max…

I hear the crunch of bones breaking. Max's bones. Crushed. By a paint can.

Guilt pierces my chest. I welcome it, along with the ugly bruises made by my seat belt. I deserve these marks. I'm foolish, negligent, heedless, irresponsible. Each adjective lashes like a whip. I have never been any of these things, yet, now, I am all of them.

Loose objects become deadly missiles in a car accident. The paint cans obeyed Newton's first law of motion: hurtling forward until one was stopped by the windshield, the other by Max's face.

A broken zygomatic arch, broken jaw. The Max news is horrifying.

Campbell comes in from the garage to where I sit in the family room, next to an untouched cup of tea. He's been to the hospital to see Jay and Carly.

"Tell me."

"It's pretty bad. They're going to wire his jaw shut to speed up the healing."

I groan and ball my hands into fists. "How will he eat? Can he talk?"

"I guess he'll take liquids mostly, stuff he can drink through a straw. Milkshakes and smoothies. They'll use a blender or use strained baby food or—"

"But how is he? How's he acting? Is he crying?"

Campbell takes out his handkerchief, blots his eyes, sniffs, sighs. I'm expecting a dispassionate report when the man before me is a heartbroken grandfather.

"Sorry, I'm sorry." The words tumble out. "I'm just desperate for information."

He blows his nose. Folds his handkerchief away. "It's awful to see him like that. His face is all swollen, so he's not talking. They're keeping him quiet. The surgery is this afternoon."

"What are Jay and Carly saying? About me?"

"Not much. I mean, it doesn't look like you caused the accident, but…" He looks away.

"But… I put those cans in there."

"Well, why did you?" He stands. "That doesn't seem like you."

I smile a bitter smile. *And there it is.*

My response is measured and acidic. "I put them where

I put them… up high and loose… because your boxes, the boxes I have repeatedly asked you to move, were taking up all the room!"

He's stunned. "So you're saying… what happened to Max… is my fault?"

"I'll take all the blame I'm due."

"You are…" Campbell shakes his head. "Un-frigging-believable. Careful, Rook. You need me on your side."

"I want to see Max."

"That's not happening today."

I'm being *handled*, like one of his wacko parents. It infuriates me. I turn away, and tighten my body, holding my legs, arms, and torso stiff and still, trying to smother the rage boiling inside me.

My anger is familiar and frightening—I've experienced it since childhood. It presents itself as a violent river pressing against a dam, seething and intense.

What am I so angry about? Being blamed? Being *rightfully* blamed? Being misunderstood? Being wrong? All I know is that I like being Good Rook. Right-thinking Rook. Straightforward and Upright Rook.

Now? If they x-rayed me, no broken bones would show.

My hurt is deep and self-inflicted.

to do list

- Buy Max stuffed elk &
  mail
- Pray for a time machine
- Call Jay and beg
- Danger: Falling ~~Rocks~~ Rook

CHAPTER TWELVE

July

Sanctuary

Church is a refuge for me.

I want to go to church today, but to my old, familiar church in Ohio. I want Jay to call and invite us down. I want Sherwin Williams to be out of Chalk paint. I want Campbell to put his arms around me and move his stupid file boxes. I want absolution and penance. I guess I want to be Catholic. Say a million "Our Fathers" to balance the scales.

None of that is going to happen. I'm mainline Protestant, I live in Colorado, my son is not calling me, and I'll be lucky if Campbell even sits with me in church, given the gulf that's opened between us. As usual, I have to make the plan. Lead the charge.

We've tried three churches since we moved. One we haven't tried, Laurel Mountain Community, has a 9 a.m. service.

Campbell and I ride halfway there in silence before I bring up the only topic I care about: Max.

"Don't you think Max is wondering what happened to me? Shouldn't he see that I'm OK? That I haven't disappeared?"

"Maybe, but you're not in charge of who Max sees. Jay and Carly are."

"This isn't right. I know Jay's upset, but this isn't fair. I need to see Jay and persuade him. Or maybe it's Carly. Do you think it's Carly?"

"I think you better back off, is what I think. Don't blame Jay. And for heaven's sake don't blame Carly. Give it time. You're always pushing."

"If they won't forgive me, I don't know what I'll do."

I do know. I'll die. My heart will break and I'll die.

"One day at a time," Campbell replies.

I want to shove that AA aphorism down his throat.

The Laurel Mountain sanctuary is simple but beautiful. We sit near the back, with Campbell on the aisle. I read the bulletin, look up the hymns, and do a quick inventory of the congregation. It's weighted in favor of older people like us. Probably the younger families go to the 11 a.m. service. The stained-glass windows create splotches of brilliant light as they filter the morning mountain sun.

The bulletin says the senior pastor, Warren Leatherman, will soon celebrate twenty-five years at Laurel. I hope he's a good speaker. What's the saying? *Sermons should comfort the afflicted and afflict the comfortable.* The former today, please.

The pews are on the hard side, and I wriggle around a bit. Two people in the narthex said hello, but no one else has been that friendly. Perhaps my stony face has put them off. I make eye contact with a little girl, jammed up against her father's side. I ache to put my arms around Max, but the dragons guarding him have said no. It feels like they are shouting it. NO!

One of the dragons is my own flesh and blood, so I'm torn between approaching him to explain myself, or putting my tail between my legs and retreating. He's a formidable dragon, so I withdraw to fight another day.

Taking in the sanctuary layout, I'm struck by the similarities between a church and a courtroom.

Pulpit. Judge's bench.

Choir loft. Jury box.

Lectern. Witness box.

Minister. Judge.

Congregation. Spectators.

In my mind, I step into the witness box, and my trial begins.

How do you plead? My inner judge points his gavel at me.

The system says I'm either guilty or innocent. I want to plead some middle ground: guilty but with mitigating circumstances, innocent but with culpability. I'm willing to be punished. I want to be punished. I also want understanding and mercy.

The gifts I withhold from others. Forgive us our debts as we forgive our debtors.

"What about intent, Your Honor? I didn't mean to hurt Max. I made a horrible mistake."

The judge bangs his gavel and, setting a record for the shortest trial ever, says, "Step down. Prepare for sentencing."

What punishment fits my crime? What is my crime?

The dragons have pronounced their sentence, and although it's crushingly unfair, part of me welcomes it. I'll suffer along with Max. For his physical discomfort and pain, I'll match that with my psychological discomfort and emotional torment.

I tune back into the service. The choir is assembling on the risers, and I watch Rev. Leatherman step to the lectern.

Go see him.

This random thought startles me, but I conclude I will go see Warren Leatherman. He looks kind, and his expertise is people in crisis. He's also an objective third party and no doubt will agree with me that Jay and Carly are being unreasonable. I'll line up my character witnesses like ducks in a row, then get Jay to change his mind. I now have a plan.

Lining up ducks is a reminder of Max and me quacking happily together as we sing Old McDonald. Can he quack now, with his jaw wired shut? Does he think his Gram hurt him? Is he tying those two things together? In the car with Gram, then BOOM. Hurt and wired shut.

I turn to the opening hymn. My throat has closed. I stand. My tears stain the page.

Biblical figures stare from the windows, eyes like flint.

to do list

- Pray for Max
- Make an actual dinner
-    for Campbell
- Research broken bones in
-    kids
- Walk or hike or
-    something — go outside
-
-
-
-
-

CHAPTER THIRTEEN

July

Bereft

What's my plan again?
I have about two minutes to figure out why the hell I'm here. I don't know this guy. I don't want to tell him what I did.

A framed poster on the wall tells me to

> Start Where
> You Are.
> Use What
> You Have.
> Do What
> You Can.

Sappy? Or profound? I can't tell the difference anymore.

"I'm glad you came to see me, Mrs. McFadden," Rev. Leatherman says, setting two cups of coffee on the table between us. "What can I do for you today?"

"Please call me Rook." Anticipating the standard confusion, I add, "My father loved chess and named all his children after chess pieces. I have two brothers: Bishop and Knight."

My personal motto is *Get to the point.* That briskness gets me into trouble, and my difficulty in apologizing keeps me there. The Rook Two-Step. I want to get to the meat of this visit, but uncharacteristically, I hold back. I decide to observe some social niceties before I dump all over the poor man. "I suspect, Rev. Leatherman, that you've run across some interesting names in your line of work."

He perks up. "Oh my goodness, I sure have. My favorite is a family in a church I pastored years ago in Oregon. All five children were named some variation of the father's name, which was Christopher. So there was a Chris, a Christine, a Chrissy, a Christina, and a Christian." He sits back, still aghast. "Can you imagine?"

We wait a beat, pondering that chaos, before Rev. Leatherman adds, "Please call me Warren, which is not exotic at all. It was my grandfather's name."

"Rev.—I mean—Warren. Sorry. I'm babbling because I'm nervous. We're new in the area, and I need to talk to someone. I picked you, so congrats on that."

"Rook, I'm happy you chose me. What's on your mind and heart?"

He lets me talk uninterrupted. *See, Campbell, this is how it's done.* He's patient when I tear up. He asks gentle questions. Talks about grief. Recommends several books. He looks pained when I tell him I can't see Max. Prays with me. Then he folds his hands across the middle of his blue golf shirt and asks, "Do you think deep down this is about the accident?" He turns his wedding ring around his finger. "Trauma can uncover long-buried emotions. You feel guilty. Ashamed. Angry. Perhaps you're struggling with deeper issues."

Deeper issues. Layers of issues, like Kleenex in a box, folded and connected. Discard grief, and here's guilt. Toss guilt in the trash, and another (t)issue, makes its appearance.

"I don't know. I don't think so." The back of my throat tingles. "I just want to live my life without causing any harm or pain. There's enough without me adding to it." My nose starts to drip, so I root through my purse for an actual tissue. I feel a strong urge to stretch out on Warren's floor and close my eyes.

"Are you angry at God?"

"No." I find a crumpled tissue and blot my face. "There are laws of nature, physics, mathematics, and if you break one, there are consequences. I'm not angry at God. If anything, I'm angry at myself."

"For?"

"For not looking harder when I changed lanes. For getting lost, which put us at that exact spot at that exact moment. For placing those cans where I did. For not practicing with Max's belt until I was an expert. It's a long list."

"Sounds like you're pretty hard on yourself. No mistakes allowed."

"I've been told I have an overdeveloped sense of responsibility. People act like it's a bad thing, whereas I consider it a compliment."

Warren nods at my weak joke. "Rook, I like to say that it's a mystery when our human understanding comes up short. We do what we can and leave the rest to God. Why don't you leave the answers to God and just concentrate on loving everyone involved in the accident, even if that's from afar for right now?"

Yeah, why not, Rook? You can't manage everything. Why the need to be in charge? Fix it? Control it? Have the answer?

"Warren, I'm obviously having trouble figuring out where my responsibility ends and God's begins. Doesn't he expect us to meet him halfway?"

Warren smiles. He holds out his hands, palms up, like they're the plates of a scale and jiggles them up and down. "Let's see. On the one hand, you have human beings. On the other, you have the Supreme Creator." He tests the scale, then spreads his hands far apart. "No. Not equivalent."

"OK, I get it."

But do I believe it?

My core belief is more along these lines: Life hands you problems and questions, and you talk to experts, read the manuals, examine the diagrams, or work the formulas to find the answers. People who know the answers are destined for success, and people who don't are destined for, well, the opposite.

If you boiled all that down, framed it, and hung it on the wall, you'd have something that looks like this:

Figure Stuff
Out Or
Suffer The
Consequences.

Another issue pops up—shame.

I wanted this visit to bring me consolation. I wanted a character witness. Instead, our conversation is highlighting my flaws and bringing me face-to-face with my worst tendencies.

Rook's Flaws
- She thinks she knows best
- She thinks she's right most of the time
- She's a slave to her internal critic and timekeeper
- She's disdainful of all the wrong-headed and lazy people in this world
- She's ashamed of these flaws

End result? I'm a strange mix of self-righteous and ashamed, critical and empathetic, sinner and saint.

A painful memory intrudes. Back in Ohio, I'd been at the grocery store, walking past the handicapped parking spaces, when I saw what appeared to be a perfectly able-bodied woman hop out of a van and start for the door.

"Hey, hey," I yelled, jogging to catch up with her. "You shouldn't park there. Those are for people with handicaps, and you look pretty healthy to me."

The woman turned, looked me up and down, and pointed back to the van. There, a man was helping a wheelchair-bound teenager maneuver off the ramp he'd lowered from inside the van. I turned back to the woman, mortified, and watched her rotate her outstretched hand, reconfiguring it to a middle-finger salute.

Sitting there with Warren, my cheeks flush. Why can't

I have a personality like my mother had, or Carly's? Warm, loving, and compassionate. Instead, I'm easily irritated, intimidating, and a bit of a smart-ass.

Warren and I talk for another thirty minutes. After a final prayer, Warren stands with me near his bookshelves. "Before we say goodbye," he says, "I have three suggestions. First, there's a group here at the church that meets every Wednesday at 4 p.m. for Centering Prayer. I think you'd find it helpful, and you'd meet some church members in a small group setting."

"I've heard of Contemplative Prayer. Is it the same thing?"

"They're closely related. Our group started a year ago, and there are usually six to ten people who come each week."

"OK. I'll try it."

"Good. Just go to the sanctuary Wednesday around 3:45 and ask for Melody. She's the unofficial leader. Second, I'd like you to look into the Enneagram. I'm going to loan you a book about it."

"What's the... Enn... what? I'm not familiar with that word."

"Have you heard of Myers-Briggs?"

"Yes, I know that one. I went to a seminar on it where I used to work."

"The Enneagram is along the same lines. It's a model for understanding your personality." He holds out a book, and I take it. "Thirdly, I'm going to give you the name and number of a local psychiatrist, Dr. Jeremy Canon. If you're so inclined, I think he could be a tremendous resource. There is one caveat."

"And that is?"

"Do you like cats?"

to do list

- Reread accident report
- Ask for current picture of Max
- Start Enneagram book
- File therapist name in a galaxy far, far away
- Try CP group at Laurel Mountain

CHAPTER FOURTEEN

August

Rebuffed

I scrunch down in my seat.

I need a little time before I knock on the door of the ranch house.

The police sent the accident report to our insurance company, with a copy to us. I poured over it, studied the diagrams, and came up relieved and frustrated by the factual muddle.

If I'm not at fault, and the other driver isn't at fault, then who is?

Even though the respective insurance companies will battle over fault, and eventually reach consensus, I need information, now. The report does contain the name and address of the other driver: Michelle Hammond, age thirty-three, of Lakewood, Colorado, and her daughter and passenger, Ashley, age seven.

"I'm going down there to see how they are," I tell Campbell, and it's like pouring gasoline on a fire.

"You are NOT," he roars, which sends Sammie into a frenzy. "That's asinine."

"I can't see Max, so I'm going there."

"Rook, no." He tones it down, but I hear the thunder rumbling in his voice. "Leave them alone. Would you want them to show up here?"

"I'm not going there to argue or accuse her of anything. I just want to see how she remembers the accident. What's wrong with going? I'll take cookies. I have to do something."

"Do *not* go there. It's a bad idea. You don't know what you're walking into." He stomps into the garage, muttering about *self-will run riot.* I recognize that AA chestnut, but he's the drunk, not me. I have my self-will on a nice, tight leash, thank you.

My self-will and I are now parked in front of Michelle Hammond's house. *Why did I come here?* I defied Campbell, but that victory faded halfway down the mountain. I picture Michelle coming to the door, a bandage around her head, telling me, "I remember now. I caused the accident. I was fiddling with the radio and didn't look when I moved over." *Vindication.*

Like Little Red Riding Hood, I've brought a gift: a basket of banana nut muffins, covered with a blue napkin. I ponder the fact that there's a lot of food associated with fairy tales— gingerbread houses, magic beans, stone soup, poisoned apples. The timekeeper in my head gives me two minutes for these idle thoughts, then sounds the buzzer.

I open the car door and stick one leg out. A little girl and an older woman come out of the house. *Her grandmother?* I pull my leg back. The woman sits on the steps while the girl kicks a soccer ball around the yard. *Is this Ashley?* If it is, she looks OK. That's a relief. A woman exits the house next to the Hammonds and comes over, bearing a casserole dish. The women chat and the neighbor returns home.

I recline the driver's seat. Close my eyes. Force myself to relax. Forced relaxation sounds like an oxymoron. I list oxymorons: jumbo shrimp, crash landing, minor crisis, and military intelligence, as George Carlin famously joked. Listing things calms me, and my breathing settles into a slower rhythm.

Why am I procrastinating? I usually meet things head-on, so skulking about here in the street is not my style. I'm procrastinating because.... *Why?* Because, here, on this side of the encounter, I can entertain all sorts of pleasant outcomes. The Hammonds and McFaddens will bond over their shared tragedy. Ashley, in a few years, will become Max's babysitter.

Once I knock on that door, ugly reality will take over. They might refuse the muffins. Throw me off the property. Call the police. I put my seat back up. *You chicken shit,* my most critical voice resounds in my head. *Get going.*

I look in the rearview mirror so that I can arrange my face into what I hope is a kind and warm look. My natural expression can sometimes be more intimidating than I would hope, or so Campbell likes to point out.

"I'm just thinking hard," I tell him.

"Thinking about what? Rounding up your enemies before a firing squad?" He chuckles, although he's closer to the truth than I care to admit.

The mirror confirms what I already know. My mouth is tight. *Not enough sleep.*

Before I can make a move, an SUV pulls into the driveway, and a man and a little boy get out. Ashley runs over and the man sweeps her up and whirls her around. Gary Hammond. I read the bumper stickers on the family car. I disagree with three out of the five. I growl and tighten my fingers on the wheel.

Gary unloads bags of groceries. Talks to his mother. Mother-in-law? The kids play with the soccer ball. Michelle doesn't appear.

Showtime.

I get out, grab my muffins, and head up the walk. Gary turns. He's in his thirties, a nice looking man with dark curly hair escaping a black baseball cap. He's wearing jeans and a Colorado Rockies T-shirt.

"Hello, Mr. Hammond?" I hold out my hand and he steps forward, smiling slightly, and shakes it. I don't set off any alarm bells. I'm another ambassador with baked goods. An older woman, near his mother's age.

"Yeah, I'm Gary Hammond. Can I help you?"

I look hard at this man, whose family is going through the same trials as mine. I want to read his expression, gauge his mood, but all I manage to deduce is that his eyes are brown and he has two of them. "Mr. Hammond, I'm Rook McFadden, from the accident? I was driving the other car when your wife and I… I hope this is a good time. I wanted to… I thought if we could talk…" I trail off. "Is Mrs. Hammond here? I brought some muffins." I hold up the basket and attempt a smile. Unfamiliar feelings—foolishness, uncertainty, ignorance, failure—wash over me.

The smile dies on Gary Hammond's face.

He adjusts his baseball cap, and his eyes flash, but whether from surprise, anger, or grief is beyond my abilities. Ashley and her brother run over, curious. "Daddy, who's this?"

He pulls them close, one on each side. Grandmother stands up from her place on the steps.

"It's none of your business," he finally replies, "but Michelle's not here. She's in the hospital. Don't you know that? Don't you know what you did to my wife?"

I stand there, gaping. "You blame me? But, the report said… My grandson is…"

"Mrs. McFadden. You shouldn't have come here." I can tell he wants to say more, but, instead, he glances down at his children and gives me a hard look.

"Mr. Hammond, the accident hurt my family too. I wish I could turn back the clock." *Ugh. Feeble and preachy.* I try again. "Both our families are suffering, and I thought meeting might make it better." *Really, Rook? What an ass you are.*

"We're *both* suffering?" Gary's tone hardens. "Really? Well, you look fine to me. Coming here, walking up to my door. Butting in. My wife. Now, she isn't walking. Isn't talking. Isn't home with her family. So how is that equal, huh?"

Gary's children stare, openmouthed, trying to follow the drama. Grandmother crosses her arms and scowls.

"I… I… didn't know any of that. I'm so sorry. Uh, I guess…" I cannot think of a single thing to say.

"Look, we don't want you here. You're not welcome." Gary raises his arm and I take a step back, but he only chops the air with his hand. "We don't want your damn muffins, or your *concern* or whatever you're peddling. Go away. Go back to—where do you live? Someplace in the mountains? Go up there and live your nice life with your nice family. Isn't that how it works? People like you will be fine, but people like us get screwed."

Gary is shooing his children up the walk away from me. The monster who hurt their mother. He has the last, harsh word.

"Stay the hell away from us. Don't ever come here again."

to do list

- Lie to Campbell about
- Hammonds
- Work on needlepoint
- Ask Jay to meet me for
- coffee

CHAPTER FIFTEEN

August

Gutted

I drive home, shattered.

At a red light, I open the car window and thrust my basket of muffins into the hands of a homeless man.

I replay my interaction with Gary Hammond. Despite his youth, he took my measure in ten seconds. He saw through my disguise of a nice neighbor lady paying a call. *Oh, have a muffin. Oh, how can I help you? Oh, isn't life just awful? Tsk tsk.* How condescending I was being—pompous vice dressed as virtue.

I sag in my seat. Campbell was right. I shouldn't have gone to see the Hammonds, but not because I should fear them. Quite the opposite. I'm the threat, with my take-charge, I'm-right, follow-me, holier-than-thou bullshit.

Writer Anne Lamott says the two best prayers are, "Help

me, help me, help me," and "Thank you, thank you, thank you." I briefly close my eyes.

Help me.

I go over the Gary scene again and again. What's wrong with me? I'm always arranging, fixing, and plotting instead of accepting.

I avoid the interstate on the way home, taking a two-lane back road I've used before. I like it because it's more scenic, but today it appeals because it's lightly traveled and I can justify my forty mph. I don't like the rental car I'm driving. I can't figure out the buttons or dials. If I am being truthful, I've lost my confidence as a driver. Gary's words thunder through my brain. I shiver. I wish I were back in Ohio. I don't have a friend in the world out here.

I recognize this as a "pity party," but I don't care. I want pity. I deserve it. I'm a good person. I truly care about the Hammonds. Gary just misunderstood. He saw a snob, a rich lady from the mountains, born with a silver spoon in her mouth.

But that's not me. If he knew how I grew up, the modest house with one bathroom, the camping vacations. I'm not a snob, but (*admit it, Rook*) I am a stiff-necked moralizer. And now also, apparently, a poor driver, careless grandmother, difficult wife, disappointing mother/mother-in-law, and unemployable project manager.

A car horn blasts, wrenching my attention back to my driving. I refocus and see, fifty yards ahead, a pick-up truck stopped dead in my lane. In front of the truck, a small herd of elk angle across the road. I punch the brake and manage to stop the car on its nose a foot away from the rear of the truck, whose driver is now leaning on his horn in anticipation of being rear-ended. Gasping, I watch the driver pile out and stride back to my car.

"What the hell, lady!" The man inspects the space between our vehicles. Satisfied that no damage was done, he gestures at the elk, who have stopped to stare at us. "Pay attention. There's always elk or deer on the road up here. You just about ruined my day."

I nod, wilting under his lecture. My hands tremble, and I nod again. The accident, and now this, a near miss. I choke out a reply. "Sorry. I'll be more careful." The last elk clears the road, the truck roars away, and I pull into the next turnout, where I sit, chest heaving, for fifteen minutes.

Has moving somehow affected my brain? I'm making bad decisions. I'm not paying attention. I'm morphing into some different version of myself, one I don't recognize. Am I losing it? I list the signs:

- I ignored Campbell to visit the Hammonds
- My driving has deteriorated from a solid B+ to a shaky C-
- I've stopped cooking
- I've given up my job search
- I'm not sleeping
- I miss Max so much I dread every sunrise

I start the car and drive home. Carefully. I watch for wild-life. I remember to slow down as I pass one particular prop-erty to see if Sad Horse is there. He is. This poor creature's paddock is dug into the side of a steep hill. The entire corral is sloped, and Sad Horse stands with one flank about fifteen degrees higher than his other. I've noticed him before and sympathized. *Looks painful. I should call the sheriff, or Animal Control, or whoever protects horses.*

I have strong reactions to animals in distress. *More than people in distress,* Campbell would say. Yeah, well, that was Before-the-Accident Rook. My empathy gene has been jolted awake and is running in high gear. I'm feeling a lot of empathy: for Max, Jay, Carly, the Hammonds, myself.

Leaving Sad Horse to his asymmetrical life, I crest the mountain and drop down the other side to my new home, Grant Falls, a village set next to a rushing creek named the Gunpowder. At 8,000 feet above sea level, Grant Falls is gritty, windy, and surrounded by towering ponderosa pines and shimmering aspens. It's stunningly beautiful—at least the part supplied by Mother Nature. The part provided by man could stand a coat of paint.

The heart of the town is a large lake fed by Gunpowder Creek and held back by a concrete dam. Gasper Lake is popular with both the locals and the Denver residents who troop up on weekends. Its glittering ripples, birdlife, and wetlands are a constant draw for hikers, canoers, fishermen, photographers, families, and nature lovers.

Right now I don't care how beautiful my external surroundings are. I'm focused on my interior.

The consensus seems to be it needs remodeling.

to do list

- Try Centering Prayer at home
- Take refresher driving course?

CHAPTER SIXTEEN

August

Retreat

Three elk stand in the meadow next to our house.

I park in the garage and despite hearing Sammie barking hysterically, I decide to walk up to our mailbox, part of a bank of boxes that serves the whole neighborhood. The bull elk swings his massive head and stares at me. The two cows in his harem look up from munching grass.

The elk count as one.

I take measured steps toward the mailboxes and study the male. He's lost a battle with a badminton net and it's tangled around his otherwise impressive six-pronged antlers. He joins Sad Horse on my list of animals in need of help.

The mail is a disappointing mix of circulars, bills, and catalogs. I think with nostalgia of the newsy letters my mother sent during my college years and early married life. She'd write

out a meatloaf recipe: "I started with a pound of ground beef."
Did she think I was going to make meatloaf in my dorm room? Or
she might describe the church altar in detail. "Mrs. Williams
gave the flowers last Sunday, a mix of daisies and carnations."
Turns out, she had excellent Mom instincts, and the details
were exactly what I craved. A visual and olfactory account of
the home life I was missing.

What advice would she give me about the Hammonds?
About Max? *Pray about it, honey. And do the right thing.*

But what's the right thing, Mom?

Dad would issue commands: "Study the board. Plan.
Avoid time pressure. Know what your opponent is doing."

Badminton Boy and his girlfriends cross to the other side
of the lane, where, apparently, the grass is greener. I walk
back to the house, careful not to step in the droppings they've
left, dainty for such large animals. The diminutive mule
deer, on the other hand, leave large piles of—what to call
it? Scat? Manure? Crap? *It's shit, Rook. Shit's a perfectly good
word.* Campbell speaking.

A black Abert squirrel darts among the rocks in the
meadow. *That's two.*

I might make the trifecta today. The trifecta is a game
I invented the first week of living in Grant Falls. I count
wild mammals, and my goal is three different species a day,
which isn't hard as we are awash in deer, squirrels, elk, fox,
coyote, rabbits, and chipmunks. We also get the occasional
bear, mountain lion, and feral cat. There've even been moose
sightings.

I'm thrilled with the elk, which isn't true of everyone.
"They're like lice," a neighbor told me. They *are* destructive,

munching on flowers and leaves and stomping through gardens, but also magnificent. I am exceedingly glad I did not run into one today.

Sammie meets me at the door, tossing a small red Kong at my feet. I throw it, hitting the doorframe into the kitchen. I put most of the mail in the recycle bin, then sit at my desk, where I search online before calling to request a welfare check on Sad Horse.

"I'm not sure that did any good, but I started the ball rolling," I report to Sammie. Talking out loud to Sammie is one reason I like having a dog around. No dog? You're talking to yourself.

I make tea, choose a small protein bar, and sit in the family room with the newspaper. Sammie crowds in beside me on the swivel rocker and chews on her Kong. The house is silent and my nerves smooth out. I decide to try some Centering Prayer. Following Warren's suggestion, I attended a session last week. Time for the home version. I close my eyes, go quiet, concentrate on my breath, and repeat the word I've selected to help stop my busy mind. *Grace,* I say softly in my head. *Grace.*

I watch my thoughts fly around: *Will life ever be normal again? Would a short vacation help my stress levels? Should we hire a lawyer?*

Grace.

The thoughts fall to the ground like deflated balloons.

Grace.

A few hardy ones re-inflate and go back into orbit. *Should I quit driving? Should I take a sleeping pill? Will Max have scars on his face?*

Grace.

They fall again. I notice one sailing toward me that looks like the Goodyear Blimp and wince. The biggie. *Will I ever be forgiven?*

I picture my Centering Prayer word firing rounds at my intrusive thoughts.

That's like the Dalai Lama manning a machine gun, or Gandhi driving a tank. Just wrong. I open my eyes. I've flunked Centering Prayer. There's no room in my brain for *peace, love, happiness.* I watch the forgiveness blimp lumber past and drift out of sight, saying, in an Arnold Schwarzenegger voice, "I'll be baaack."

"Probably in the early morning hours, like 4 a.m.," I sigh and tell Sammie. Sammie indicates that a game of fetch will fix everything. I indulge her for ten minutes, managing to hit a table leg, the glass-fronted bookcase, a lamp, which stays upright, and Sammie's water dish, which upends.

My dad loved baseball, and I learned enough lingo from him to know that, right now, in my life…

I'm batting zero.

to do list

- Send Max that funny
- duck card
- ID my Enneagram Type
- (also for Jay, Carly, &
- Campbell)
- Turn, turn, turn

CHAPTER SEVENTEEN

August

Debrief

C ampbell and I circle each other like boxers, wary and alert.

I used to enjoy this time of day. The debrief. After Sammie gets over her hysteria at a strange man entering the house—*Oh yeah, it's you. I remember you now!*—we talk over the day's events, sharing our victories and defeats. We advise each other, laugh at the other's stories, defend each other's intentions, and plot against common enemies. We're comrades. A team.

Now, more out of habit than desire, we're sitting with two glasses of iced tea on the deck. I listen to the sounds of a late summer afternoon. A truck downshifting on the parkway. A siren. Doors slamming. Kids yelling. I pull Sammie onto my lap.

"How was school?"

"OK. I'm learning the kids' names." This is Campbell's

secret weapon. Parents are thrilled when the new principal says, "Hello there, (insert name). How are you?"

"Has anyone stepped up to be *that kid*?" He knows I mean the kid who will take up huge amounts of his time and make his life miserable.

"A first grader named Scotty is in the lead. He went berserk today. Scratching, biting, and kicking. He punched a kid, called his teacher a bitch, and tore up the office."

"Gosh. What'd you do?" I stroke Sammie's silky ears, more soothing than prayer beads.

"I suspended him for a day. I'm not a fan of suspension, but we all needed a breather. I like Scotty, the little shit, but I need time to meet with his parents and teacher, and figure out the resources available for him, and make a behavior plan. He's going to need a lot of support." Campbell frowns and chews on his thumb.

I picture myself in that situation. Nope. Not my strong suit. Proving that I gravitated to the right career, and so did Campbell, whose motto has always been: *What can we do to be helpful to children?*

I look at the ridge of mountains visible from our deck. They're blue and soft in the afternoon light, but I know up close they're brown and flinty.

Campbell swirls his ice cubes. "To feel better, I went down to the kindergarten room. This one kid looked at me and asked, 'Are you going to die soon?'" He laughs. "I must look ancient to a five-year-old. What'd you do today?"

I study the deck, which needs to be sanded and stained. I brace myself. Stall. "I called about that horse. The one who has to stand slanted? They promised to check it out."

"So, you called about the horse, and…?" His tone implies that I need to account for another nine hours and forty-five minutes.

"If you must know, I went down to the Hammonds." I'd considered withholding this information, but I'm not a good liar, and besides, I'm an adult and can make my own decisions. *Even if they're bad ones.* "It didn't go particularly well."

The silence stretches out, and I can hear Campbell breathing heavily.

"God, Rook. That pisses me off." Campbell sets his glass down, hard. "We talked about this repeatedly. I asked you not to go. That Hammond guy could, could…"

"He didn't do anything, except tell me to take a flying leap." I don't mention my near miss with the rental car.

He's shaking his head and his voice gets louder. "The Hammonds are not your problem. I'm sorry about the Hammond woman, but according to the report, she wasn't wearing her seat belt. Normally you'd be all over that, how it was her own fault." He sees he's scored with that. He's right. I pass my judgments around like salted peanuts at a party.

Campbell is on a roll, doing that escalation thing he's so good at. I react in the precise manner that infuriates him and guarantees further escalation. I pull inside my shell and go mute. I'm a turtle, and he's a kid poking me with a stick, threatening to turn me over. We've developed this melodrama over the years, and we're quite good at it.

"You've gone off the rails. I don't understand you. I want to defend you, but you're making it difficult." He stands, his face stiff, and goes inside.

"Thanks for the support," I call to his retreating back.

Moments later I hear the front door slam and see him striding down the lane.

Sammie yelps in pain. Looking down, I realize I'm no longer using her ears as prayer beads, but as stress balls, and snatch my fingers away. "Sorry, girl."

I dissect Campbell's speech, probing for any truth. I concede that we discuss the Hammonds too often, but the rest of it is bullshit. "He can pound sand," I say out loud. Some helpmate. "In sickness and in health, right Sammie?" Campbell is the one who brought our marriage to the brink. Even though that was years ago and we survived it, he has some nerve to point a finger. A few weeks of weepy behavior on my part is not on par with the king-size damage he, and his drinking, had done.

We got married a week after college graduation, with my older brother Bishop officiating. It was a muggy June day, but I was oblivious to the weather, to the guests, to the flowers, the music, and the cake. I just wanted to be Mrs. McFadden and spend one glorious day after another with my smart, handsome husband. His drinking didn't bother me. It was just an extension of what had gone on in college, where most of the guys, and plenty of the girls, got drunk regularly.

It took ten years for me to realize how miserable I was. I'd grown used to his stopping after work for a few drinks and going to bed while he stayed up. I didn't notice his blurry stare as he made yet another Manhattan. I engaged in the arguments, overlooked the bad driving, and ignored the hangovers. Parties were the worst. I had to wait until he was ready to leave, and he was never ready because there was always more drinking to do.

"Not yet," he'd say, and weave off to the bar.

Our marriage resembled the myth about how to boil a frog. If you just plop it in boiling water, it jumps right out. But if you put it in cool water and gradually increase the heat, the frog stays put, getting comfortable at each new temperature until it's too late. I know this has been debunked and is not scientifically accurate, but it's a useful shorthand for what was happening. We were dying by inches, and we were clueless.

He came home increasingly later, picked fights, and would yell at a bewildered two-year-old Jay. He had unsavory friends. Not to mention the fit he threw if there wasn't going to be liquor available when we went out. He was surly. He lied. He became mean. Although I didn't know the language of AA then, we were all sliding down to Campbell's rock bottom, the turnaround point, where he'd be fed up with his behavior and get help.

Following a wretched party where we didn't get home until 3 a.m., and I watched Campbell drive off with the terrified teenage babysitter, I made an agonizing decision. "Jay and I are leaving," I told him late the next morning when he finally came down to the kitchen, unshaven and snarling. "This is not the life I want. You're not the father Jay needs." I couldn't say the word divorce out loud; it was too humiliating. What a failure. The competent Rook McFadden would wear a scarlet D on her chest for the rest of her life, but at least I could protect Jay.

An hour later, Campbell threw two suitcases in his car and roared out of the driveway. He rented an efficiency apartment and continued his downward plunge. I knew about his low-life friends, the drunk driving, the poor work performance, and the fact that he'd broken the second, seventh, and eighth commandments. Or was it the third, seventh, and tenth? I never pressed him for the details of his lowest point, but he hinted it was a combination of self-destructive, dangerous, and illegal behaviors that drove him to his first Alcoholics Anonymous meeting. Three months later, Jay and I welcomed him home with balloons and banners. Maybe he was just, as AA said, *sick and tired of being sick and tired.* He hadn't had a drink since.

"AA meetings are better than church," he told me. "I've never been in a group where men are so honest about their emotions and failings." He liked the atmosphere: "Bad coffee, salty language, great jokes."

The teachings and mottos of AA became the touchstones of our lives. They shaped how Campbell made decisions, how he dealt with relationships, how he went about his job. *Let go and let God. One day at a time. The Serenity Prayer.* Was alcoholism an illness or a weakness? Who knew or cared? It was a scourge and AA was the vaccine.

I stand and go to the deck railing, where I spot Campbell several lanes away, taking our usual route through the neighborhood. He's nursing his anger, preparing his arguments, girding for battle.

He'll bring volume and vulgarity to the fight, but I have the big guns.

I'm logical and relentless.

to do list

- Try Centering Prayer
- again
- Send Carly flowers
- Let the sunshine in
- LISTEN to Jay! Don't
- be pathetic

CHAPTER EIGHTEEN

August

Purgatory

I watch Jay approach the coffee shop with mixed feelings.

My first reaction is to admire his physicality: his easy stride, athlete's body, confident manner. He's a good-looking man, six-foot-one, with intense blue eyes and hair the color of the latte I'm about to order. My second reaction is fear. This has to go well. I'm not a good card player, and Jay is. I peek at my cards. They're all the same: *I'm your mother.*

When John Jefferson McFadden, our first and only child, was born in 1976, the country was swept up in a bicentennial fever. I guess we were caught up too, naming him after two of the founding fathers: John Adams and Thomas Jefferson. We called him by his first and middle initials so often, we finally landed on the nickname Jay. Except for a couple of years when he was a surly teenager, we'd always been a happy band of three. We wanted another child, and I would get pregnant easily, then have a miscarriage. *Secondary infertility.* Poor Jay was destined to be an only child. Because of this, he got the full attention of two parents with high expectations and plenty of opinions. He survived, though. He got good grades, had lots of friends, and was easy to discipline, as his motto was, *If you can't do the time, don't do the crime.*

"Hi, Jay. Thanks for meeting me. Can I buy you a coffee?"

He doesn't hug me, but that's not unusual. He's carved thirty minutes out of his workday to see me, and I sense the tone of our get-together. All business. *OK. I can do that.*

We sit with our coffees at a table in a corner. I'm grateful there aren't many customers this Wednesday morning, and I get to the point: "I don't understand why you're keeping me away from Max. I'm desperate to see him."

I've read enough in the Enneagram book to know my son is a Type Eight, which is The Challenger. It's classified as the powerful, dominating type who is self-confident, decisive, willful, and confrontational. That's good if you want him to be the striker on your soccer team. Or sell your product. Or defend the Alamo. Bad if you want to talk about feelings.

I'm not surprised when my Type Eight son hits the ball directly back to me. "You have no idea what it's like at our house right now. It's a shitstorm."

"Tell me. What's it like?"

"Max has totally regressed. He won't sleep alone, so we have him in our room, where he needs to be anyway because we have to watch him constantly. If he would throw up in the night, with his mouth wired shut? He'd aspirate the vomit and die."

103

Jay's eyes and words are in sync. Cold and sharp. "Nobody's sleeping much. Then when he's up, he's mopey and clingy and—did you know he won't get in the car now? So that's a major headache."

I stare at my son. His fury is like another person at the table. I open my mouth to speak, but Jay plows on. "Carly's taken a short leave from work, but she may have to ask for some significant time off. Her mother's coming to stay and help, so Carly at least can go to the store or the gym. She needs a break."

"Jay, let me do that. Please. I'm here and I want to—"

"No." Jay looks me directly in the face, and his eyes glitter with emotion. This I can read. *Resolve.* "I'm so angry with you. Carly too. What you did. It was about the most..." He pauses while we both fill in the blanks. *Stupid. Irresponsible. Thoughtless.*

"So you're never going to forgive me?" I say this carefully, neutrally. I'm moments away from breaking down in this public place, and I tighten my body, willing myself to hold it together.

"Mom." There's anguish in his voice. "I'm not ready to answer that, so don't ask me—someday. I don't know. Maybe. Not now for sure. It's taking all my strength to go to work and keep things going at home. Support Carly. Be there for Max. Handle the doctor appointments. Deal with his moods. Her moods. My moods. There's no room for you."

Only two seats left in the lifeboat. He's assigned them to Carly and Max. *Good man.* Someone raised him right. *Oh yeah, I did.*

"Max..." Jay's voice breaks. "Max is my priority now. The doctors say another inch and he'd be dead, or brain-damaged for life."

We sit with this, in silence. *Could have, would have, should have.* Jay circles back. "I want to know something. Max came part-way out of his shoulder harness." Jay demonstrates, violently thrusting his upper body forward, and I shrink back. This is new information. "That put his face in the path of the can that clocked him. There's only one reason he'd come out of his belt like that."

I hang my head, bare my neck for the executioner, and whisper, "I didn't make it tight enough."

"Damn straight. Not tight enough. Rule One."

I look at Jay through tears, but he's looking at his watch. This meeting, this interview, this interrogation is over. My "I'm your mother" cards are useless, and I fold. Grief sweeps me away.

I consider driving to Jay and Carly's and camping on the lawn until they let me in, embarrassed by the wild-eyed woman on their front porch. What do they want? Remorse? Revenge? A pound of flesh? I'll cut out my heart. I'll be meek as a lamb. I'll do whatever they want.

As long as it doesn't include exile.

to do list

- Stop crying!!!! You big
-     baby
- Pray (at least try)
- Stitch — order purple
-     thread
- Find a friend — maybe
-     Cheryl from   CP
-     group?
- All you need is love — True?
-
-
-

CHAPTER NINETEEN

August

Despair

I sit in my bedroom, broken.

My meeting with Jay, that I hoped would be the first step toward reconciliation, has turned into a fall down a mine shaft. I've cried, read my Bible, prayed, and watched the tops of the ponderosa pines sway outside the window. I'm out of plays.

Ice clinks in the refrigerator downstairs. The printer in the office makes a soft chuffing sound. Hudson whirs past the door. Hudson, named after the butler on *Upstairs, Downstairs*, is our robot vacuum. He emits soft musical chimes and posts plaintive messages on his small screen: *Please free my left wheel. Please clear my path. Please charge my battery.* I think humans should display such messages on their foreheads. It would prevent a lot of confusion. *Please feed me. Please get me some aspirin. Please give me a hug.* Right now my message would flash: *Please forgive me.*

My thoughts turn to Max. I picture him asleep in his crib. Modern mothers don't put anything in the bed with baby, so he's stretched out in his footed pajamas on a fitted sheet. No stuffed animal friends. No pillow. No blanket. I clench my teeth shut and experiment with how it feels to have your mouth wired shut. *It feels awful. Is he losing weight? Is he forgetting how to talk?*

I long to be standing there, rubbing his back, but the doctors recommend he heal with just mom and dad around. Comforting figures he doesn't associate with the accident. I disagree, and usually would share my opinion, but not now. Not after I saw my totaled car at the lot. Not after I read the accident report. I want to blame Michelle, but my memories are hazy, dream-like, unreliable. One thing is clear: Max was in my care that day, and now, Max is suffering.

I think about blame and percent of blame. I have well-developed skills at finding fault, assigning fault, and, even occasionally, my inner voice concedes, *being* at fault. I've been reading the Enneagram book Warren loaned me. I think I know my type, out of the nine possible. I'm Type One: The Reformer. The rational, idealistic type who is principled, purposeful, self-controlled, and perfectionist. *How does that help?* My "principled perfectionism" and "rational purposefulness" have landed me in exactly the same place as if I were any of the other eight types.

I tell myself bad things happen, everyone's life contains tragedy and sorrow, but it's to no avail. I'm caught in a cycle of regret, grief, and self-recrimination.

I try Centering Prayer again. Close my eyes and begin. *Grace.* Immediately, my conversation with Jay fills my head, and it's like trying to escape from a bombastic party guest. Jay's harsh words have *Grace* pinned in a corner. Poor *Grace* tries to get a word in edgewise but is too polite to interrupt. I should change my CP word to *SHUTUP.*

I crave peace and quiet. I'm glad Campbell doesn't want to retire for a few more years, because once we're both home full-time, quiet will be hard to come by. He'll read me some news bit from the computer, want help finding an extension cord, announce he's going to paint the front door or suggest going out for coffee. All good and noble activities, but they'll be on his timeline. These are unworthy thoughts; the poor man works hard and deserves to retire. *Just not quite yet, Lord,* I pray.

Sammie, jammed between me and the arm of the chair, watches the treetops out the window. She growls at some birds congregating there. "Sammie, be quiet." Really, how can I get this dog to simmer down? It drives Campbell crazy. "I'm just not a dog person," he says. I get it. I even smile at his outrageous comments, like when he took the plastic dry-cleaner's bag labeled DO NOT GIVE TO CHILDREN off his laundered shirts, waved it in front of Sammie's nose, and asked her, "Shall I put your Kong in here, sweetie?"

I realize Hudson is dinging and has been for some time. Stuck somewhere, and calling for roadside assistance. *We interrupt CP for these important announcements.* I check the first guest bedroom but don't spot him. I usually find him beating his little head against a baseboard, overcome by the fact that two walls have come together to form a right angle.

I pause outside the room where Max naps. The dinging is louder. Hudson is under the crib, one wheel off the carpet, choking on something. I pull the crib away from the wall, stoop, crawl, reach, and pull out a stuffed pig, its ears stained and flattened.

When Campbell gets home from school an hour later, he finds me there, limp from crying, clutching Mr. Pig, Sammie curled next to me like a tiny comma. He lays down the law. "You're going to see that psychologist, psychiatrist, whatever—that the minister recommended. You're going because you're… you're not… acting like yourself. You're scaring me."

I'm scared too.

to do list

- Stop crying... stop lying
- Walk around the lake
- Unpack some boxes (or
- repack and move to
- Australia)
- Send Jay the story about
- the bears in Aspen

CHAPTER TWENTY

August

Q&A

"**T**his isn't my first rodeo, you know."

I sound defensive, but I don't care. He's a psychiatrist. He'll figure it out. Dr. Canon has been practicing in Grant Falls for thirty years. He's an oddity as a Freudian—whatever that means. I took two psych courses in college, and all I remember are Pavlov's dogs and Maslow's hierarchy of needs. But Warren Leatherman recommended this guy, and Campbell basically told me to "get thee to a nunnery," so here I am. Freudian, schmeudian. I just want to feel like my old self.

I'm shocked to find out Dr. Canon wants me to actually lie down on his couch. I settle myself on his sofa. I'm tense. Unlike the dentist's office, there are no cutesy posters on the ceiling. I decide to take control and talk for fifteen minutes straight, describing the move to Colorado, my frustrating job search,

AA, Campbell's new job, the accident, not seeing Max, and my uncharacteristic response: sadness, tears, anger, grief, guilt.

"You said this wasn't your first time in therapy. How would you characterize your past experiences?" Dr. Canon finally gets a word in edgewise.

"Semi-successful. It was marriage counseling, by the way."

"What worked?"

"*I* worked. I learned a few useful techniques."

"So what didn't work?"

Campbell, I think, but don't say out loud. "Let's just say my husband and I have had the same argument for the past thirty-nine years, so there's that."

The scene I'm in is straight out of a made-for-TV movie but with lower production values. Dr. Jeremy Canon, bearded and holding a notebook, in an armchair. Me on a couch, feeling ridiculous. Vulnerable. A tad angry.

"And that argument is about?"

"Getting asked lots of questions that have obvious answers. Kind of like now." My hostility boils up, cooking my words leather-tough.

"What questions does your husband ask? Are they existential? To kick off a lively discussion?" Dr. Canon is unfazed by my ire.

"You mean like, 'What is the nature of good and evil?' Or 'How many angels can dance on the head of a pin?' No, they're more along the lines of, 'Have you seen my glasses? Where's my wallet? Is my mother's birthday on the sixth or the eighth? What's the Wi-Fi password? What day is Thanksgiving on this year?' and so on. By the way, the answer to that last one is Thursday."

"He's asking for help, and you don't want to give it."

I bristle. "I don't want to give it when it's the millionth time I've answered that question. We've just assumed these roles over the years, right? He gets to be clueless, and I have to be all-knowing. I'm tired of my role."

"Is he tired of his?"

"Why would he be? How cool is it to not clutter up your mind with details? I'm his encyclopedia, personal shopper, accountant, travel agent, quartermaster, tech support, keeper of all passwords—you get the idea."

"Have you discussed it with him?"

"One hundred million times."

Silence.

"A number of times."

Silence.

"Many times. And he promises to do better, and then we slip right back into the old pattern."

"Have you always felt this way?"

I consider this for several long moments. "I guess not. It must have worked for many years, but now it's like being in school all the time. Having to perform. Have the answers. Never let him down."

"And what would happen if you didn't know the answers?"

"Nothing. He's told me to say, 'I don't know,' but usually I do know, so that feels like a lie. Then I have to watch him floundering around, opening drawers, going through my files, and wasting time. I feel mean, although it can be satisfying. There. I admit it. I enjoy his discomfort. I'm horrible." I wait for my therapist to disagree, but he doesn't.

"Can you tell me a role Campbell plays in the relationship where he's the one with the answers? Where you rely on him?"

114

I think. "He's in charge of all the remotes. I know zip about them. He understands all the stuff in the garage and how to start them and what kind of oil and gas they use. He keeps track of his doctor appointments, his prescriptions, and his haircuts. He always buys me wonderful gifts. The sales ladies are impressed with his skills."

"You're telling me he really sees you and knows what you like. It's important to him to please you."

"Yeah. OK, Dr. Canon. I know it's unfair, after all these years, to alter the balance in our marriage. I was happy being the know-it-all and he liked that arrangement. Now I feel resentful and under-appreciated. He probably feels confused and let down. What changed? Was it the accident?"

"Was it?"

I fume. "I think I'll try your techniques on Campbell. When he asks me 'Where did I put my passport?' I'll say, 'How do you feel about losing your passport?' Answer every question with a question. There—problem solved."

Dr. Canon is unruffled. "Was it the accident that changed the dynamic between you and Campbell?"

"I don't know. Maybe we're just getting more entrenched in our poor behaviors as we age. There's an AA saying: 'Wherever you go, there you are.' Basically, you can't run away from yourself. We get older and our personalities harden like cement. Does that make sense? The accident just exposed what was happening. That's why people get divorced even after twenty or thirty years of marriage, isn't it? Some trauma or change exposes the rotten foundation."

I feel a ripple under my hand. Ziggy the Therapy Cat is thrusting his head under my fingers, wanting attention. When

I called Dr. Canon to make an appointment, he explained that seventy percent of his patients were fine with Ziggy, twenty percent were allergic and wanted him kept out of the room, and the other ten percent went elsewhere, preferring cat-less therapy. I'm not allergic and don't care. If Dr. Canon wants to be a living stereotype, fine by me.

"Tell me more about Campbell. How did you meet?"

"I met him the first day of college, standing in some line. We started talking, and something clicked. Turned out we were in dorm buildings next to each other, so we would walk to classes together, get coffee, and talk. That's always been the secret sauce for us—being real with each other. Sharing." Tears roll down my cheeks.

"Describing that has made you emotional. What are you feeling?"

I sob. Dr. Canon waits. Ziggy ducks under the couch.

"Lonely. Alone. We aren't talking like that anymore."

"Why not?"

"We're mad at each other. The blame game. He probably blames me for insisting that we move here. He has a new job and needs to focus on it. I'm all needy and weepy instead of what he expects: strong and supportive. I blame him for not forcing Jay to let me see Max. I blame him for putting his damn boxes in the back of the car."

"How could you change that dynamic?"

"Why do I have to be the one who changes it?"

"Do you like how it is?"

"No."

"I imagine you've been a leader all your life."

I think of my high school and college yearbooks, studded

with clubs and activities. If it moved, I was president of it. "Yeah. I like to run things."

"So, lead."

The good Dr. and I spend the rest of the session talking about my childhood, my marriage, and my current anguish. I can't pick up a theme or a thread. I don't hate being here, but I'm confused. This is an expensive chat, and I want homework. A rubric. A "To Do" list.

Instead, I get an appointment for the following Tuesday.

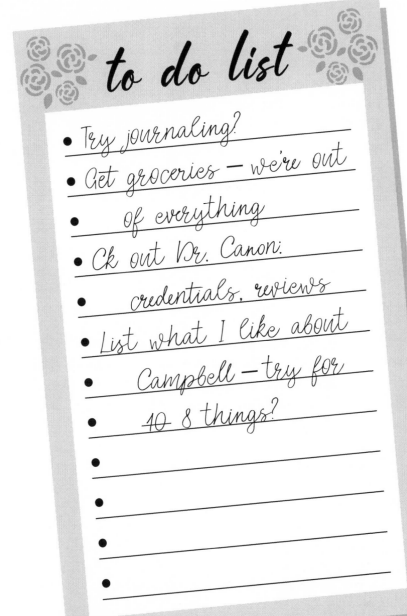

to do list

- Try journaling?
- Get groceries — we're out
-   of everything
- Ck out Dr. Canon:
-   credentials, reviews
- List what I like about
-   Campbell — try for
-   ~~10~~ 8 things?
-
-
-
-

CHAPTER TWENTY-ONE

August

Setback

I treat myself to grocery shopping after therapy.

I like this chore—wandering the aisles, reading labels, spotting new products, eating the samples. I learned years ago never to go with Campbell, who pilots his cart like a pirate captain, sideswiping and broadsiding other carts as he executes his assault-and-plunder style. His mission? Get in, liberate the food being held hostage, and get out. I'm about reconnaissance and scouting. The gender gap on full display in aisle five.

At home, I put away the groceries, figure out dinner, and balance the checkbook. When the phone rings, I jump and glance at the clock—4:30 p.m.

"Hello, sister dear." My brother's rich bass voice enfolds me, and I smile at his standard opening.

Bishop Franklin Brownlee is older by five years, an ordained Presbyterian minister who has served the same church in Dublin, Ohio for the past nineteen years. He's levelheaded and funny and, unlike me, finds his chess-related name a source of amusement. "Too bad I'm not Catholic," he points out. "Then I could aspire to become Bishop Bishop Brownlee." The Presbyterians have elders instead of bishops, so his name gets no traction with the Frozen Chosen.

"Hello, brother dear." My spirits lift. I like talking to my brother. He's a good listener, like Rev. Leatherman, but when I talk to Bishop, I can swear and call him names.

"I've been thinking about you. How are you?" he asks.

"OK." I picture my sigh traveling to Ohio and whooshing into his ear, leveling his smile into a straight line. I blink away the tears that have formed in my eyes.

"I want to hear more about that, but first, some sad news. I'm sorry this call isn't going to cheer you up. It's about Uncle Howard. He died earlier today."

I lean back. Whimper.

"I know. I know."

Uncle Howard is our mother's brother. We've adored him since we were children. "Let's go to the zoo," he'd suggest, holding out the candy jar from his credenza. Or he'd scoop us up to go to the park, or swimming, or a movie.

I recall one of my favorite Uncle Howard memories. I was seven that Halloween, and two days before Trick or Treat night I developed the flu. I cried and pleaded with my mother to let me go out. I had the best costume ever—Minnie Mouse—replete with mouse ears, the enormous polka-dot hair bow, the swirly dress and outsized matching shoes, the white gloves, and billowing bloomers. But my mother would not relent, and I stayed in bed, my costume draped over a chair. Even Bishop's offer to share some of his candy did little to cheer me up.

Four days after Halloween, I was over the flu but not over my disappointment when the doorbell rang. "You answer it," my mother called from the kitchen, so I dragged myself to the front door, opened it, and gasped. There stood a six-foot-tall Mickey Mouse, holding out a white-gloved hand and saying, "Minnie, would you do me the honor of stepping out with me tonight?"

The rest of the evening was magical. I had my Minnie outfit on in five minutes, and Mickey, otherwise known as Uncle Howard, and I were whisked by a hired car around town. First, we went to dinner, then to a roller skating rink, then to a penny candy store where I was allowed to fill my Halloween bag to bursting.

Uncle Howard had a serious side as well. He gave us our first jobs, working at the warehouse and office at Buckeye Brands, the company he started after serving in WWII. We did odd jobs: sweeping up, cleaning the coffeepot, stapling reports together. He inspected our work, paid a fair wage, and didn't let us goof off because we were related to the boss. Howard and Aunt Catherine's only child, Christopher, died of leukemia when he was two, so they bestowed lots of love and attention on the Brownlee kids.

"Were you with him?"

"No. I was going over there later this week to take him out to dinner. His housecleaner found him. It was quick. Heart attack."

"What an absolute peach of a guy."

"The peachiest."

We go silent and I study a picture on the wall. It's of Bishop and me with our mother and Uncle Howard at a family Christmas gathering. Howard's wearing an elf hat.

"When's the service?"

"There isn't going to be one." Sammie wanders in and puts her paws on the front edge of my chair. She makes a feeble attempt to jump up, feigning helplessness. I pick her up and place her across my knees, stunned by Bishop's announcement.

"It's what he wanted. I'll be working with his lawyer to tidy up his estate. He named me his executor, you remember." Bishop laughs. "Hey, I thought of a great Uncle Howard story. One summer when I was in high school, he proposed a challenge at the driving range. Said if I won, he'd take me to King's Island and I could ride the roller coasters there all day long. I was a pretty good golfer so I said absolutely. What I didn't know was that he was friends with the guy who owned the driving range. Howard went out there ahead of time and placed one of his balls at the extreme end of the range—200 yards. Acted all innocent when he won. Of course, he confessed immediately and took me to King's Island anyway."

I smile. Uncle Howard loved pranks, which were never unkind but sometimes annoyed me. Then again, I'm not the prankster sort. "Good story. The world lost a kind soul today. If there's anything I can do, or should do, let me know."

"I'll email you Howard's obituary. It'll run in *The Columbus Dispatch* in a couple of days. By the way, did you know Howard's middle name was Harrison? Howard Harrison Rawlings."

"I didn't know that." A wave of regret rolls over me. My

mother's only sibling is dead, taking with him bits of family history and stories, now lost forever.

"I do want to talk to you about how you are, about Max, anything you want. Shall I call tomorrow? Right now I have to get this obit up-to-date and send it to the paper and call the cousins about Howard."

"No, do your executor thing. Call whenever you have time."

I don't tell him that I'm surrounded by lifelines that seem just out of reach—Rev. Leatherman, Dr. Canon, Centering Prayer, the Enneagram.

I'm going to drown, despite all these good-hearted efforts.

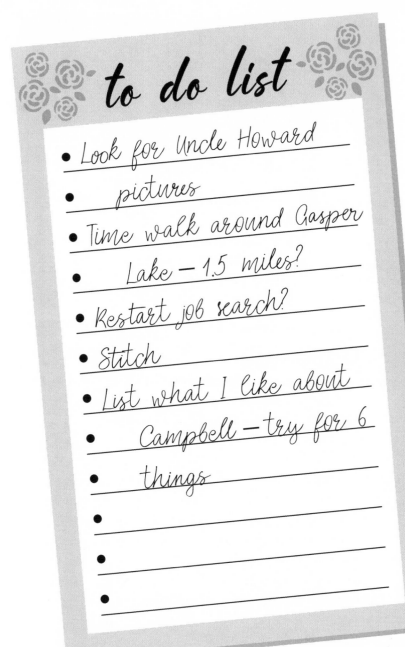

to do list

- Look for Uncle Howard
- pictures
- Time walk around Gasper
- Lake — 1.5 miles?
- Restart job search?
- Stitch
- List what I like about
- Campbell — try for 6
- things
-
-
-

CHAPTER TWENTY-TWO

August

Unfair

I'm like Goldilocks.

Dr. Canon has several upholstered chairs and a couch, and I've tried them all, searching for a spot that's *just right* so that I can unburden myself more easily.

Today I return to the couch, sit, and pick up the bottle of water the doctor has on the table. It's next to a box of tissues. *That makes sense. Cry it out, rehydrate, cry it out, rehydrate.* Ziggy slips from under the couch and glides into my lap, where I pet him automatically.

Dr. Canon is in his usual place, a Queen Anne chair in a blue and white herringbone pattern, holding a notebook and pen, letting the silence build up.

"Dr. Canon," I begin. "It's interesting that your name is church-related and you're in the confessional business. Like a baker being named Baker."

"Not many people notice that."

"So here's my confession. I'm guilty. I confess. I want to pay the price. But… I just want the price to be… I guess the word I'm after is 'fair.'"

I hear Dr. Canon shift in his chair. Tap his pen on the notebook he never writes in. "Fairness. How would that look?"

I tighten my grip on Ziggy and his purring stops. He gives me a chilly look and jumps down, disappearing behind the desk in the corner.

"I've done, and do, a lot of good things in my life, but they don't seem to count anymore. I stayed with my husband even though he put me through the wringer. I'm a conscientious employee. I support my church. Tithe. Vote. Volunteer. I love my son and daughter-in-law. Adore my grandson. Happily pay taxes. Salute the flag. Mow the grass. Plant trees. Drive a hybrid car. In other words, I'm a model citizen, wife, and mother."

Dr. Canon's trick—keeping quiet so that I'll speak—works again. I babble on. "All that—not enough. Out the window. One slip and the world crashes down on me. That seems unfair."

"You put a lot of energy into meeting the world's expectations."

"Of course. That's what makes things go smoothly. In fact, that's my general assessment of others. I feel like telling them: *Make an effort, people!*"

I try to gauge how this ugliness is affecting Dr. Canon. I plunge on. If I'm paying to have my head shrunk, I might as well get my money's worth.

"You know how they say schools should teach kids critical thinking skills? I have those, but not the way they mean it. I just think a lot of critical things about people."

"Tell me about your parents and their expectations of you."

A memory flashes. I'm in the church basement, resplendent in my scout uniform. Holding up the three middle fingers on my left hand, I pledge, along with the other girls, "to serve God and my country, to help people at all times, and to live by the *Girl Scout Law*."

"My parents were wonderful," I tell him. "And their expectations were entirely consistent with the 1950s. Obedience, duty, respect, hard work. I delivered. In aces."

Dr. Canon offers a statement rather than a question. "In my field, we would say you have a very strong Super Ego, that is, you've internalized a set of cultural rules, mainly through the guidance and influence of your parents or other authority figures. The Superego aims for perfection and controls our sense of right and wrong and guilt."

"I drank the Kool-Aid, you mean."

"An excellent summary. Pithy."

"I know I'm a little uptight if that's what you're saying, and I'm all right with that. I've made peace with my rigidity. I'm not sure how that's related to my current feelings, about Max, and all the rest. Why am I so sad? Weepy?"

"Rook, I'm a Freudian psychoanalyst. It's my opinion that your current state of depression and anxiety is caused by a conflict between your conscious mind and unconscious mind."

"Depression and anxiety? Those are strong words. I'm just a little sad and upset. I don't like being described as depressed and anxious. That's not me."

"You're having a forceful reaction to those descriptions. Why?"

"Because that's not me!" My voice—my debater, amateur actress, presenter, manager voice—goes up in volume. "I handle stuff. I solve problems. I deal with the world as it is. I don't retreat and get depressed. I refuse to be that person. All I want from you is some help regaining my perspective so that I can move forward."

"Is movement the only solution? What else could you do instead of move?"

I let out an exaggerated breath. "I'm remembering something about chess my dad taught me. The rook only moves straight forward or sideways, never on the diagonal. After I grew up, I thought that was a pretty slick coincidence, because that's how I move. Full steam ahead! To answer your question, yes, I think movement *is* the right solution. Otherwise, you sit there stuck."

"I believe we can get you 'unstuck' by bringing that unconscious material into your conscious mind. The accident is a trigger to a hidden place inside you, and I believe that's why you're reacting so strongly and struggling to cope. I want to intensify our efforts to help you explore that trigger. Are you willing to keep digging?"

I nod. "Sure, I'm willing. But can we bring in a backhoe instead of using shovels?"

Dr. Canon isn't offended. "I'll move it along as fast as I can. There are some techniques we can try at future sessions. But to round out the hour today, tell me about your relationship with Campbell."

I pull out my notebook and read some entries aloud. "We argued about him losing some receipts, we fought about him chewing his fingernails, we had words about me forgetting to put gas in the car, and we had a good time watching a TV show together. That's three fights and one good time, so I guess it's seventy-five percent bad. I'm using up a lot of wife points."

"Wife points? What are those?"

"It's a theory I made up, probably inspired by the fact that I worked at a bank. Husbands and wives build up points in their marriage bank accounts when they do nice things for each other. For example, bake your husband's favorite cookies? He adds points to your account. Surprise him with a new shirt? He gives you more points. Complain he left his shoes in the middle of the bedroom? That's a deduction. Marriages work when the account stays positive. You can run a deficit for a while, but not long term."

My personal marriage bank balance is still positive, but I've been making hefty withdrawals since the accident. But hey, back when Campbell was drinking heavily, he'd been the one bleeding his account dry.

When the session ends, I actually feel a little better.

Not $125 better, but better.

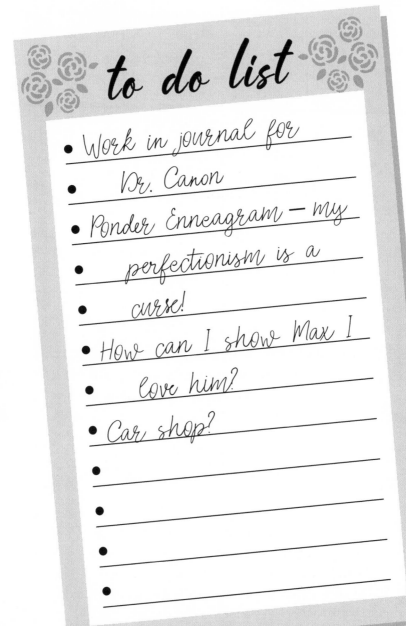

to do list

- Work in journal for
- Dr. Canon
- Ponder Enneagram — my
- perfectionism is a
- curse!
- How can I show Max I
- love him?
- Car shop?
-
-
-
-

CHAPTER TWENTY-THREE

August

Flight

The phone in the office rings and Sammie erupts.

I grab her as I race past so that I can shut her up and hear. "Hello, sister dear." Bishop. Good.

"Hi. How are things in Ohio?"

"I have interesting news. Howard pulled a fast one. When I sat down with his lawyer to go over the will, I found out that he left his money to various charities and organizations, but his house to us!"

"Us? You mean the cousins?"

"No. Us. The two of us. Bishop and Rook. His favorites."

"Well…" I frown and stroke Sammie's ears. "Huh."

"I know. One last surprise for the Brownlee kids. There's no mortgage either. We're supposed to go through the house and take whatever we want before the rest of the contents go to an auction house. Then we'll put it on the market." Bishop pauses. "Unless you want to move back to Ohio and live there."

For a brief moment, I toy with that idea. Running away from the mess I've made in Colorado. Back to the heartland. Living in my uncle's house with Sammie. Getting my old job back. Six-year-old Rook likes the idea. Sixty-two-year-old Rook knows better.

"No, I'll pass. What about you? You've been living in church-owned housing all these years. Maybe you're interested."

"No, it's not right for us."

"Will it be easy to sell?"

"It's in a good location and in pretty good shape. It might need a little work. Hey, I want you to come back here and help me. The estate will pay for your flight, and you can stay here with us. Come back and go through the house with me. Pick out some mementos. Plus we have an assignment from Uncle Howard we should work on together."

"Assignment? That doesn't sound good."

"Do you want to know now, or when you get here?"

I sit up straight at my desk and enjoy a foreign emotion— pleasure. "I'd love to come. And keep the assignment secret." A burst of energy surges through me, and I recognize it instantly. It's the thrill of starting a new project. "Thanks for the invitation. I'll book a flight and let you know the details. Love you."

"Love you back."

I almost ask about his book but stop myself. His book is a sensitive topic. His concept is to pull together headlines from marquees outside churches. He's gathered hundreds of them, maybe even thousands, but struggles with how to edit and arrange his collection. By topic? Season? Denomination? State? He has a title: *Made You Look! Witty, Wise, and Wacky Sayings as Seen on Church Marquees Across the U.S.*

What he doesn't have is a book. Busy with sermons, funerals, weddings, budgets, and meetings, he never finds the time. "But on the bright side," he once told me, "I have a twenty-year supply of good stuff for Woodbridge's marquee."

I hear Campbell pull into the garage, then come into the mudroom. Sammie hurls herself toward the intruder, but I don't get up or intervene. Let him run the Sammie gauntlet. He appears in the doorway of my office. "Hello. How was your day?"

"All right. I saw Dr. Canon. Worked on Max's Christmas stocking."

I'm halfway through my current needlepoint project, stitching a giant stocking for Max. I picture all of us—the five of us—gathered around a beautifully decorated tree, while Max pulls gifts out of his new stocking. Everyone is laughing and happy. *The Spirit of Christmas Yet To Be.*

"Listen to what happened at school. I was talking to a fourth grade mother in my office when the police came in and arrested her for car theft. The very car that was out in front of the school!"

It's a good story, but I barely nod. We go silent, circling the elephant in the room. I go first. "Did you talk to Jay today?"

"Yes. I called him at lunchtime." Campbell pauses, and I exercise one of my most underworked muscles: patience. "He says Max is doing a little better. They're taking him to a child psychologist and working on his fears using play therapy. On the plus side, the doctors say they might unwire his jaw in a week or so. Kids heal fast."

"Am I still *persona non grata*?"

"I suggested coming down Saturday, but they're taking Max on a weekend trip if they can get him in the car. They could use some fun." Campbell clears his throat. "I have some other news related to the accident. Turns out my secretary's daughter lives in the same neighborhood as the Hammonds. The neighbors have been helping out with meals and babysitting, so they get updates on Michelle."

I wait.

"Michelle's in a rehab facility right now. She's been diagnosed with a traumatic brain injury."

Every word of that phrase is horrific. "What does that…?" I trail off.

"I don't know much about it. I did a little research and people with TBI—that's what they call it—can be emotional. Difficult. Illogical. They suffer confusion and mood swings. It's rough."

I recall Gary, Ashley, the little boy, and the grandmother. The elephant in the room—my not getting to see my grandson—shrinks to the size of one of Max's stuffed animals. Gary's right. They did get screwed.

Campbell tries to pivot, but his instincts are lousy. "How was your therapy? I have my doubts about that guy. A cat? Really? You could find someone else. It's like getting a sponsor in AA. Not everyone's a good fit."

"I don't want to start over with someone else." For a reason I can't name, Campbell's suggestion is irritating.

"Why not? Is it the money? If you don't like the guy or his cat, find someone else."

"The cat is fine. It's you who doesn't like cats, or dogs." *Or, at the moment, me.*

"So? What's that got to do with, with…?" I stare at him, and he surprises me by going silent.

I know what he's doing. He told me about it the other evening. One of the guys at AA pointed out that when a cop stops you and reads you your rights, one of those rights is the infamous, "You have the right to remain silent." Jerry thought that ought to apply to husbands, which got a big laugh from the men.

The doorbell buzzes, and Sammie goes berserk. Shushing her, I sprint to the door. The nondescript man on the porch holds out an envelope, and I instinctively take it. Satisfied, he stands back and delivers his iconic line in a bored voice.

"You've been served."

to do list

- Pick memento from
- Howards house
- Drive by our old house
- Get Max a Buckeye
- souvenir
- Arrange coffee w/ Ellen,
- Diane, Meg
-
-
-
-
-

CHAPTER TWENTY-FOUR

August

Arrival

Bishop is late, and I seethe.

I've been standing at Passenger Pick-up at Columbus International Airport for ten minutes. Scanning for Bishop's car again, I'm getting hotter, thirstier, and more annoyed with each passing second. A large RV rumbles to the curb, blocking my view. I cross my arms and crane my neck. Where *is* he? Counseling some poor soul in distress? How about my distress?

The driver of the RV hops out and comes toward me, materializing from a dim shape into my brother. I'm confused. Bishop drives a beige sedan and, as far as I know, has never been interested in driving into the sunset in a "Rustic Rambler."

My brother is tall, six foot three, so I've spent my life looking up to him—physically and emotionally. He's teased me, protected me, ignored me, bullied me, laughed and cried with me, and said the words that pronounced Campbell and me husband and wife.

Bishop closes the distance. I look down, surprised by a prickle of fear.

I've been eager to sink back into the familiar, easy relationship Bishop and I have always had, but now I'm not so sure. I bite the inside of my mouth. What does he think about the accident? Does he want to protect me or set me straight? Soothe me or give me a tongue lashing? He's perfectly capable of either, or both.

He pulls me into a one-armed hug and grabs my roller bag.

"What's this?" I point to the RV. "Youth Group camping trips?"

"Nope. It's ours. Get in and I'll tell you about it."

I settle in the passenger seat and look over my shoulder. A table with bench seats, a small sink, a two-burner stove-top, cupboards. "So… what's the story on this RV?"

"Barb and I are starting to think about retirement in two or three years. We saw this for sale and decided to try it." He waves at the dashboard. "Do you like it?"

I'm more a Marriott kind of traveler, but I fake an enthusiastic reply. I picture living with Campbell for weeks on end in a space the size of our kitchen and family room. "Can I just squeeze past…? Oh sorry, are you using…? Oops, excuse me…. I just need to get in…. Can you turn that down…?" Our marriage would crumble in a month.

After Bishops parks the RV in his driveway, I say a quick hello to my sister-in-law, Barb. Then I rejoin Bishop, who's eager to demonstrate how the table and bench seats turn into a bed and the entire bathroom is a shower stall. Like Barbie's Dream House, it's fun to play with, but I wouldn't want to live there.

I notice the license plate. "You got a vanity plate."

"Yeah, I thought it'd be fun. A conversation starter at the campgrounds."

"REV 41. Occupation plus your birth year. Yep. Knowing you're parked next to a minister ought to get the party started. You know, I spend a lot of time at traffic lights trying to figure out vanity plates. I saw one the other day: OH RLY. First I thought it was the owner's name—O'Reilly—then it hit me that it probably said 'Oh Really.'"

"Or it really was O'Reilly." He delivers this deadpan.

"Ha. I tried a vanity plate once—RMNS828—Mom's favorite verse. Romans 8:28. God works all things together for the good…"

"…of those who love him," Bishop finishes. Mom said it hundreds of times. Her touchstone verse.

"I've been trying to apply that verse to my life these past few weeks," I confide, "but I'm not having much luck. Want to hear the latest? The Hammonds—that's the name of the woman in the other car who was ejected—they're suing us. Well, technically, our insurance company and us."

My brother clucks and furrows his brow. "That's gotta feel bad."

"It feels every kind of bad." I try to go on, but I choke, swallow, and clench my fists. *What the hell?* Bishop disappears inside the RV and brings me a cup of water. While I drink and cough, he inspects latches and handles on the RV's exterior.

"You OK? No Heimlich needed?"

I shake my head. Stare at the RV's license plate. *Ohio. Birthplace of Aviation.* Take a deep breath. "Bishop, I've run away from home."

"I know. We can talk about it if you want."

"I'm not sure you can help. Things are kind of a mess."

My brother doesn't answer. He deals with messes every day. Broken, unhappy people looking for help, forgiveness, and direction. His presence is an invitation to "come as you are." I prefer presenting a polished, professional exterior. I step to Bishop and pat his arm. "I'm glad to be here. You're just the tonic I need. And speaking of tonic, any chance you could offer me one, mixed with a little vodka?"

"It so happens I am offering a drink special today." He looks at his watch. "Yes, Happy Hour has begun. Let's get inside in the air conditioning."

"Before we go in, I've been meaning to ask. How are the Abernathys?"

Bishop groans.

Gene and Olive Abernathy are long-time members of Bishop's congregation at Woodbridge Presbyterian. They have Strong Opinions. Abernathy anecdotes range from amusing to aggravating. My favorite is when they came to Bishop concerned about two naked male cherubs in a small stained-glass window in the vestibule. They wanted him to order new stained glass that would dress the tiny angels. He finally solved the problem by shoving a tall table topped with a silk flower arrangement in front of the offending bits.

"The Abernathys are alive and well. They're in California visiting their daughter and pondering their next move. You know how they say what doesn't kill you makes you stronger?

Gene and Olive are going to kill me, but the good news is after my death I'll be put up for sainthood—a first in the Presbyterian Church."

The RV tour over, I go into the kitchen while Bishop takes my bag to the guest room. "Barb, can I help with dinner?"

I look to see if Barb is wearing one of the aprons from her extensive collection, and I'm not disappointed. This one has a big green pickle on the front with the tag I'M KIND OF A BIG DILL. My sister-in-law peers into a saucepan. "No. I got it. I'm making teriyaki chicken and rice."

"Sounds delicious." I sit at the kitchen table and pick up Calvin, Bishop and Barb's ancient dachshund. Cal licks my ear and settles his head over my shoulder. I inhale his doggy scent. *Yum.* Bishop returns from his bellhop duties and starts setting up glasses and bottles on the kitchen counter.

"Hey, bartender. Could we continue our talk after dinner? I'm obviously in need of your advice."

"Brother hat or minister?"

"Uh. Mm. I guess brother."

We both know what that means.

Less hand-holding and more ass-kicking.

to do list

- Email Campbell instead
- of calling
- Go over Howards will?
- Get chicken recipe from
- Barb
-
-
-
-
-
-
-

CHAPTER TWENTY-FIVE

August

Consoled

"**W**ould you like to take a walk? The humidity's bearable this time of night."

I'm grateful for Bishop's invitation to get out of the house later that evening. Two minutes later we're headed down the sidewalk. In the dark and not face to face, it's easier to confide. When Jay was on a travel soccer team, we'd spend weekends driving to tournaments. Our taciturn teenager would open up there in the backseat, in the dark, with the miles flashing by. We'd talk and share, the radio soft in the background.

"I envisioned this perfect life where we'd move to Colorado and live happily ever after. I'd bake chocolate chip cookies and be Max's favorite grandmother."

"And the deer would come to the door and eat from your hand."

"Ouch." I half turn to him. "Did you flunk counseling in seminary?"

"You said brother hat, not minister. *Wait upon the Lord.* That's minister. *Quit yer bitching.* That's your brother."

We stroll in silence for half a block. Insects hum in the heavy, warm air. Street lights dab splotches of light onto the sidewalk. "I find it hard to wait, and bitching is one of my best skills. I've never felt so in the wrong. It's hard for me to be wrong."

"I know. You have high standards, and that's a good thing. The world needs that. Just don't appoint yourself judge, jury, and executioner. It's not a good look."

I blink back tears and search for a tissue in the pocket of my shorts. "I've cried more in the past month than I have in my entire life. Well, that's not true. I cried a lot when Campbell was drinking."

I got through that. I'll get through this.

I wonder if there's a twelve-step program for people in my condition. Which is what, exactly?

Bishop stops walking. I do too. He turns and, mimicking E.T., gently puts his index finger on my chest. "Be wrong. Be human. Be imperfect. Be God's child. Loved. As is. Be my sister. Loved. As is. Wife, mother, mother-in-law, grandmother. Loved. As is."

I blow out my cheeks. *Loved. As is.*

I'm more apt to believe: *Loved. As if.*

We continue down the block, and Bishop says, "I've talked to Jay, you know. I've called a couple of times."

"Well, sure. I mean… of course."

I stumble over a piece of broken sidewalk. People are drifting away from me. Jay. Campbell. Bishop. I chastise myself for having such unkind thoughts. It isn't a competition. *But if it were…?* Who wouldn't side with Jay, Carly, and Max?

"I'm seeing a therapist."

"How's that going?"

"Sometimes I like it, but mostly I want to knock his block off."

"It's going well, then."

I can't help myself. I snort. "Good one." I continue to giggle as we swing around some trash cans and head back.

"It wasn't that funny."

"No, but I want to reward your comedic efforts. I miss laughing. Which reminds me, we should talk about our plans for Uncle Howard and all that. It's why I came here, you know. Diversion and entertainment."

"Oh, there'll be plenty of that. We'll kick off the festivities by visiting Howard's lawyer tomorrow morning. I'll let him explain our assignment. We can go through the house the next day."

We finish our walk reminiscing about Howard. I remind Bishop of the Halloween caper, and he surprises me with a story I've never heard.

"Do you remember Ranger?"

Ranger? The image of a mottled brown, black, and white streak of fur with one ear up and one ear down presents itself. "I think so. He was Mom's dog, right? When I was in elementary school. What about him?"

"One weekend Mom and Dad took you somewhere. I begged to stay home, told them I was old enough to manage on my own. I was fifteen. I promised I'd be responsible and nothing would happen. I had a couple of friends over on Friday night, and one of those knuckleheads left the door open and Ranger ran away."

"Oh no! Poor Ranger. I mean, poor Bishop. What did you do?"

"I looked for two hours, then called Uncle Howard, who swooped in like the cavalry. He came over, and we started a systematic street-by-street search. We looked for that stupid dog the entire weekend. Uncle Howard called his friends in the police force, he helped me make dozens of posters, he called shelters, he spent hours driving and walking around yelling, 'Ranger, here Ranger.'"

"You obviously found him. Where?"

"Sunday afternoon we came home, defeated. I was ready to be grounded for the rest of high school, but the worst part was going to be Mom's tears and Dad's icy looks. Guess who was sitting on the front porch, licking his rear, covered in burrs?"

"You dodged a bullet there, my friend."

"Don't I know it! What I'll always remember is Howard holding me by the shoulders and telling me, 'This will remain between the two of us.' He never mentioned it again. He was just there when I needed him."

Oh, Uncle Howard, who's there for me now?

to do list

- Don't get Barb an apron
- as hostess gift! ☹
- Drop by old job (bad
- idea?)
- Ck out "naked angels" @
- Woodbridge!!!!
- Buy Sammie new Kong
- Cook dinner for B/B or
- take out
-
-
-

CHAPTER TWENTY-SIX

August
Challenge

"Mrs. McFadden, Rev. Brownlee. Welcome."

Bernard Cole ushers us into a conference room. Neat stacks of stapled documents sit on the table in front of three of the high-backed chairs. Off to the side, there's a coffee service set up next to a plate of pastries and doughnuts. Bishop selects a bear claw, pours a cup of coffee, and settles into one of the designated chairs, facing me across the broad, polished table. I look the offerings over, calculating calories. I can't see anything under four hundred, sigh, pour a coffee, and sit down. Mr. Cole, in his mid-fifties, with a round face and a tailored suit that doesn't quite hide his expanding stomach, takes the end seat between us with his own coffee and a croissant.

"First, I want to tell you how much I liked and admired

your uncle. What a wonderful man! He and my father met at Rotary years ago and became great friends, as well as golf and poker buddies."

Bishop nods. "Your father schooled me in a round of golf a few years back, but I've tried to suppress that memory."

Mr. Cole tells us to call him Bernie, and we all agree to proceed on a first-name basis. "The firm has handled Howard's legal affairs for, oh, forty-odd years. We took care of both the personal and business sides until Howard sold his half of Buckeye Brands fifteen years ago. But enough of the suspense: Let me spell out the major bequests in your uncle's will. He left $20,000 each to his nieces and nephews and his two living sisters-in-law. He left $200,000 for Rotary Club projects, and on his instructions, we'll be throwing a party for his bowling league in a couple of weeks. He also left $500,000 to endow two scholarships for members of The Ohio State University Marching Band. It was his favorite organization, as I'm sure you know."

Uncle Howard's love of the band? Everyone knew about that. As a child, I loved wandering around the "band room" at his house, which was the den decorated with band memorabilia: framed sheet music, glossy coffee table books, postcards, cartoons, parts of uniforms, signed programs, video and audiotapes, and even his trumpet from 1939. It was a mini-museum for The Best Damn Band in the Land, also known as TBDBITL.

Bishop smiles. "What I remember is Uncle Howard watching the OSU games on TV, marching around the room with his trumpet, playing along with the band."

I'm not a big football fan, but I've been to a few OSU

games, and the marching band is impressive. Legendary. The crowd eats up everything they do, but the fan favorite is the famous Script Ohio, with a senior sousaphone player dotting the *i* in Ohio. Script Ohio, first performed in 1936, is the band's quintessential formation, their signature move. From a block O three deep, the drum major appears, and leads the band, single file, in a constantly flowing script, as if a giant hand was writing the word Ohio on the green of the football field. The effect is mind-boggling. The highlight, of course, is when the drum major and a senior sousaphone player break from the script and strut to the point on the field above the letter *i*, where the drum major points to the spot and the sousaphone player sweeps off his or her hat, "dots" the *i*, and bows deeply to both sides of the stadium.

Bernie nods. "Howard always said that being in the band was one of the highlights of his life. The band, marrying Catherine, and starting Buckeye Brands after the war—he was proudest of those three things."

I do some mental math. "Wow. Those are large gifts. I guess I didn't realize how much money Uncle Howard had."

"You've heard the phrase the millionaire next door? That was Howard," said Bernie. "No frills. He drove an older car, didn't take flashy vacations, and made conservative investments. And of course, in addition to the cash bequests, there's the house, which he left to the two of you. It's paid off, and I estimate it's worth about $300,000. Net of fees and expenses to sell it, you each should receive about $130,000 or so." I glance at Bishop, who has a ghost of a smile on his face.

Bernie puts down his pastry, wipes his hands, and straightens the edges of his papers. "Howard did have a special assignment for you two. It's not a prerequisite to inheriting the house; it's just something he thought you'd have some fun with. It has to do with scattering his ashes. He didn't want a service but liked the idea of you picking a place that was—" Bernie picks up his sheaf of papers and searches through several before finding what he wants. "Here it is. And I quote: 'appropriate, meaningful, and fun.'"

I picture Uncle Howard pulling a quarter out of his ear. "So that's the assignment. Well, speaking for myself, it'd be an honor. I'm just relieved he didn't send us on some crazy mission, like riding bicycles across Ohio dressed as clowns, scattering his ashes in every county." I feel an inspiration. "I could take them back to Colorado and scatter them on a mountaintop."

Bishop shakes his head. "That wouldn't be meaningful to Uncle Howard. He wants excitement and flair. Like throwing them off the top of the Magnum roller coaster at Cedar Point or spreading them around the ninth hole at Muirfield."

Bernie gives a thumbs-up. "Those are both good. Definitely in the spirit of what he had in mind. Ohio law says that once a body is cremated, it's considered legally disposed of. Buried, so to speak. Where the ashes go after that is strictly up to the family members." Bernie looks from Bishop to me. "Your uncle did have one idea about his ashes. It's…" Here the serious, middle-aged attorney starts to giggle. As the giggles intensify, I'm afraid he's going to snort coffee up his nose. "You ready?"

We nod and Bernie leans back. "He thought if you could manage it, that he'd love to have his ashes scattered at an OSU football game. At halftime, while the band is performing."

Bernie searches our faces. I don't have a poker face, so I'm sure mine is saying, "Are you nuts?" We both turn to Bishop. He's gobsmacked but manages a question. "The Horseshoe? Under the eyes of 100,000 fans? There's no way." He brightens. "Unless you already got permission from the university? In exchange for the band scholarship money?" Bernie shakes his head no.

"But, Bernie," I reach out to touch his arm. I'm a "toucher," and Campbell has warned me that people don't always appreciate a pat on the back, arm, or knee. I draw my hand back. "I am literally and figuratively a Girl Scout. I have always obeyed my parents, my teachers, the police, and almost everyone in a position of authority. That certainly includes campus security. I can't see running out onto the field with an urn full of Uncle Howard."

"See, this is exactly the sort of spirited conversation Howard envisioned. Talk it over. Get creative. Howard's cremains are currently at the Sadler and Cross Funeral Home in Upper Arlington, so you'll need to go down there and pick them up. Here's their business card, my card, and the key to Howard's house. Let me know when you've taken whatever items you want from the house. And please, call me with any questions or concerns." We spend another twenty minutes reminiscing about Howard, then Bernie escorts us out.

Standing in front of the elevators, Bishop breaks the silence. "I knew about scattering the ashes, but that last bit was unexpected. I have a 1 p.m. meeting at church. Let's sit down after that and talk, OK?"

I nod. Howard's assignment is silly. I've got grown-up concerns to deal with, and this last joke from my nice but goofy uncle is not what I need right now.

I'm looking for solace, not slapstick.

to do list

- Take Barb and Bishop out for dinner
- Get Kreinik gold thread — needlepoint shop
- Try CP again — ask Bishop if he knows it
- Find out why Calvin doesn't bark

CHAPTER TWENTY-SEVEN

August

Strategy

The naked angels are a hoot.

I visit Woodbridge's vestibule to see the cherub genitalia that upset the Abernathys. Turns out it's about as offensive as seeing a naked three-month-old. I go out the front door to read what Bishop has put on the exterior church marquee. It says, LET YOUR PAST MAKE YOU BETTER, NOT BITTER. I sit at the pipe organ keyboard, wishing I hadn't quit piano lessons when I was fourteen. I stand in the pulpit, study the windows, and finally plop down in a pew. I sit very still, close my eyes, and let the peace of the sanctuary fill me up.

I like churches. Also temples, cathedrals, synagogues, mosques, and chapels—basically any place of worship. I see the appeal of monasteries and convents, too. Order, silence, routine. A uniform. The singing.

Michelle Hammond pops into my head. I suck in my breath. I haven't thought about Michelle since arriving in Columbus. Max? *Constantly.* Michelle? *Not so much.* Is that a good thing or a bad thing?

"Sorry, Michelle," I whisper, "Hope you're having a good day." It's wonderfully quiet. My breathing slows.

Bishop finds me there twenty minutes later. "You look content. I'm free if you want to talk."

I trail him back to his church office, where I open the discussion. "I appreciate that Howard liked the stadium for his final resting place, but let's rule that out, OK? We're not *Ocean's Eleven* material."

Bishop surprises me. "I'm telling you, Rook, $130,000 will go a long way toward my retirement. I could even upgrade the RV. Howard was very generous to us, so shouldn't we try to fulfill his last request?"

"Are you serious? Are you saying we should actually give it a go?"

"Yes, I am. Let's try to scatter the ashes at the Shoe. If we hit a snag, then we fall back on other options. Nothing illegal. I'm against getting my name in the newspaper."

I picture the headline.

LOCAL MINISTER BURIES UNCLE AT THE SHOE

I think of Campbell and how he has a basic rule about publicity: It's all bad. Even the good is bad. Whenever he considers a course of action, he imagines how it will look in the newspaper.

PRINCIPAL LOCKS 3RD GRADER IN
CONFERENCE ROOM

PRINCIPAL SUSPENDS STUDENT FOR
GUN MADE OUT OF CANDY

His rule has served him well, and it seems Bishop operates under the same one.

"Right," I say. "A low-profile operation. Leave no footprints."

"We could find someone to do it for us."

"Bribe a band member."

"Let's say incentivize, not bribe," says Bishop. "When the police find our notes in the dumpster behind the church, I want them to be the least incriminating possible."

I snigger. "So find a college student who needs money and has a slight bent toward criminal behavior. That's probably easy to do."

"Or one of us creates a diversion while the other dumps the ashes."

I have a brainstorm. "What if it could be part of the half-time show? Maybe they're shooting a canon, or there's smoke from a train or fireworks—something like that? Shoot the ashes onto the field."

"We're flailing here. We need facts. I'll ask my choir director if she has any connections to any band members."

I agree to conduct some online research and go sit at a computer used by the youth director. I discover that OSU gives ninety-minute guided tours of the Horseshoe for $75 and sign us up for the next open slot two weeks out. The tour includes the Steinbrenner Band Center.

When I re-enter his office, I see Bishop has picked up the rosewood chess piece that sits on his desk and is rolling it around in his hand. It's not part of a set; it's the unique gift Dad presented each of us on our twelfth birthdays—a bishop for Bishop, a knight for Knight, and a rook for me. They're about two inches tall and exquisitely carved.

"For luck?" I motion toward the bishop in his hand.

"Not really. Just reminds of Dad, and he wasn't about luck."

"True. He was about rules and consequences. I can hear him now." I assume a gruff voice. "Remember Rook, plan your moves in life. Know the endgame."

Bishop looks at me with sympathy. "I imagine it feels like you've lost control of the board right about now."

"Thought we were talking about Dad," I mumble. "I hate it when you use chess metaphors."

"I'm a preacher. Metaphors are my meat and potatoes. There, see how I did that? Used a metaphor to explain how metaphors—"

I interrupt. "Cut it out, Bishop. Just because you're a minister and my older brother doesn't make you the fount of all wisdom."

He presses his lips closed. He puts his thumb and index finger to his mouth and makes a twisting gesture as if turning a key in a lock. Good. I've shut him up. I want his advice, but he knows me too well. All the buttons to push. All the skeletons in the closet. I feel a wave of appreciation for Dr. Canon, who I can keep at arm's length. I can't help adding, "In fact, Dad told me once that the rook is a major piece. It's stronger than the bishops or knights, which are minor pieces. Take that, Mr. Minor Piece."

My brother comes around his desk and puts his arms around me. I hold out for a moment, then relax into his embrace.

Sometimes you just want to be held.

to do list

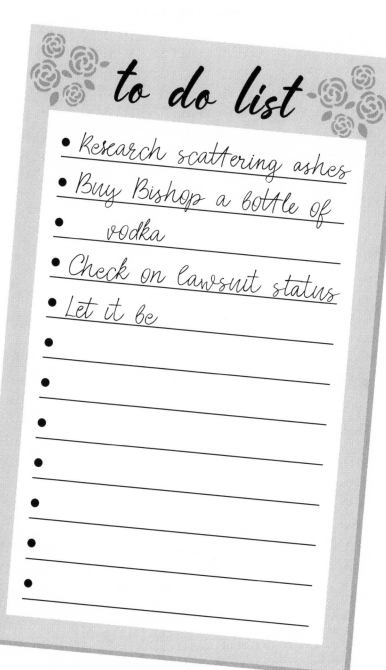

- Research scattering ashes
- Buy Bishop a bottle of
- vodka
- Check on lawsuit status
- Let it be

CHAPTER TWENTY-EIGHT

August

Retrieval

"I t's not how much we gather that matters; it's how much we scatter."

From behind the steering wheel, my brother reads from an index card. "That's the thought for the day, courtesy of Wellspring Lutheran Church in Topeka, Kansas." Bishop gives me a sidelong glance. "How much we scatter. Get it? Cause we're going to scatter Howard's—"

"I get it. Hey, why are we in this RV? Strikes me as over-kill for a trip to the funeral home."

"Barb's going up to Mansfield to visit her sister, and my car's getting a brake job, so don't mock my ride." He backs out of the driveway, the RV beeping. "We'll get the ashes today, then tomorrow we can go through Howard's house. Sound good?"

"All good. That quote you just read, is that going in your book?"

"Probably. I was thinking, I might ask Woodbridge for a sabbatical. I could take a couple of months, drive the RV to a remote site, and knock the book out. I could use Howard's money to self-publish if I can't get a publisher interested. Think Woodbridge would go for it?"

"After almost twenty years of faithful service? They'd better. Your book will sell like hotcakes in every Christian bookstore in America. I'll buy a dozen myself."

"I am not worthy."

We roll toward Upper Arlington, catching every red light. I finally break the silence. "Do you think Uncle Howard accomplished everything he wanted to in life?"

"His was a life well lived. He was respected, kind, and knew love."

"You reach our age, and you start to think about what you've accomplished, and how you should spend the time you've got left."

"Isn't that why you moved to Colorado? You chose family."

"Which is ironic, because if I'd stayed here, there wouldn't be a rift in the family."

"Don't second guess yourself. I imagine it's less of a rift and more of a…"

"A gulf? A rupture?"

"I prefer hiccup, or interruption. Give Jay time."

"That's kind of my point. You never know how much time you have left. So you shouldn't leave things unsaid or undone. That's why people make bucket lists, isn't it? Do you have one?"

"A bucket list? Oh, there are a few things I'd like to do. Ride a mule down the Grand Canyon, finish my book, give the opening prayer in the U.S. Senate. You?"

"Hmmm." I ponder his question. "I'd like to visit the top twenty art museums in the U.S., and now that we live in Colorado, maybe climb a fourteener. I also need a new chocolate chip cookie recipe. My Ohio recipe is a total failure at 8,000 feet."

"What's a fourteener?"

"That's a mountain over 14,000 feet. Colorado has fifty-some of them."

"Maybe they could haul you to the top *in* a bucket."

"Haha. Yours sound doable, except the Senate thing. I do have an idea about your book, though. Why don't you shoot for something smaller? An article? Something you could submit to a magazine."

"So, not a bucket list, but a 'buckette' list?"

"Exactly. A teeny-tiny bucket with small, modest items." I pause, considering my real wish list. "Those things I just mentioned? Those are just filler. There's only one thing I want: back in the good graces of Jay and Carly."

"Which is something you can't control."

"That seems to be the message the universe is sending me." I switch gears again. I need to dodge all this brotherly love—*smotherly love*. "I suppose you've been present at a lot of deathbeds—people's final moments."

He turns serious. "Yes, I've been the watchman many times, and it's always powerful and mysterious."

"Have you ever preached a sermon about heaven?"

"No, I don't want to wade into that. My views would be

unpopular. For example, I don't believe that people will be reunited with their spouses, or children, or pets in heaven." He frowns. "I don't think human relationships will be on the agenda at all. Loving God is the purpose of life—here, and in heaven."

"But people want to believe they'll see their loved ones in heaven because that's what brought them happiness on earth. Who wants to hang out for eternity with a bunch of folks you don't know?"

Bishop turns into the driveway of the Sadler and Cross Funeral Home, a handsome brick building with copper trim around the windows. A hearse sits in the circular drive.

"Remember the movie *Beetlejuice*?" he asks me. "At the end, Beetlejuice is in the waiting room of the afterlife. He's holding a paper printed with his number in line, the type you get at the deli counter. It's some ridiculous number like nine trillion, and he looks up and sees that the number being served is three. Plus, he's sitting next to a witch doctor. I love that."

I grin as he parks under a shade tree. "That was funny. Endless waiting and being stuck with some weirdos in a small room. My definition of hell."

Bishop turns the key and opens his door. "Human relationships are the opportunity we get to practice loving, kind of a trial run for the main event: loving God."

"I think I need a lot more practice."

My brother gets out, then leans his head back in the RV. "That's why we have that gift called grace. Now let's go collect Uncle Howard."

Larry Sadler is a charming host, if "host" is the right word for the occasion. He leads us to a conference room equipped with a coffee machine more suitable to a Starbucks. While he makes a skinny latte for me and a mocha cappuccino for Bishop, I survey the room.

Mahogany table, excellent chairs, pale blue walls, soft lighting. I glance at the art: a seascape, a mountain vista, horses galloping through a meadow, sunlight dappling a redwood forest. Whatever your vision of heaven, it's depicted. There's no picture of a waiting room with plastic chairs and a "Serving number 3" sign.

"Mrs. McFadden, Rev. Brownlee, please make yourselves comfortable." Larry Sadler places our drinks in front of us and sits across the table, looking quite comfortable himself.

"First, let me express my condolences on the death of your uncle. I didn't know him personally, but his obituary was very impressive. He was clearly an outstanding citizen and business leader."

Bishop takes the lead, having dealt with many funeral directors in his line of work. "Thank you, Mr. Sadler. He was certainly all of that, but to us, he was just a warm and loving uncle. I assume all of your expenses have been covered by Mr. Cole?"

"Oh yes, that's all taken care of. Ah," and here he looks at us with a kind smile, "currently the cremated remains are in our most basic container. I'm afraid it's little more than a heavy cardboard box really. Perhaps you'd want to consider a more elegant or permanent urn? We have beautiful styles: wood, metal, glass. Most people are surprised by the variety and artistry available."

Bishop jumps in. "We'll be scattering the ashes according to my uncle's final wishes, so a permanent container isn't necessary."

If Mr. Sadler is disappointed, he hides it well. "I understand that Mr. Rawlings was a devoted Ohio State fan. Do you have a moment? Regardless of your plans to scatter the cremains, I think you'll enjoy seeing this."

We follow him through a nondescript door in the corner of the room into a large display room filled with caskets, which stand with their lids raised to show off plush linings. I stroll along, touching the sleek metal and wood exteriors, admiring the handsome fittings and handles. Ahead, Mr. Sadler waits beside one particular model.

It's a casket designed for an Ohio State University football fan, an über-fan. It's scarlet and gray, of course, with a large block **O** sewn into the satin lining on the casket lid. The handles are shaped like footballs, and the pillow for the deceased's head sports a block **O** as well. I wonder if it plays one of the band's most popular fight songs, "Hang On Sloopy," on a continuous loop throughout eternity.

"Isn't it something?" Mr. Sadler pats the smooth gray finish. "We just started carrying these two years ago, and we've had eight families choose that casket for their loved ones."

I widen my eyes at Bishop behind Mr. Sadler's back, mouthing "OMG." We murmur our thanks and return to the conference room. While Mr. Sadler leaves to fetch Uncle Howard's cremains, I notice some brochures on an end table and thumb through them to pass the time.

"Bishop. It says here you can get your ashes sent into space. Or you can be mixed with paint and an artist will create a painting using your, ah, your, ah…"

"Basic chemical compounds?" Bishop doesn't seem surprised. "I've heard of that. I also think you can be made into a bullet, or put inside a locket, and I'm certain there are other freaky possibilities." He looks thoughtful. "Weren't Hunter Thompson's ashes fired out of a canon up in the Rocky Mountains just a while ago by his friend Johnny Depp?"

"You're right. I'd forgotten. Should we take notes? Could we use any of these ideas?" I stuff the brochures in my purse as Mr. Sadler returns.

"Here we are." He places a container about half the size of a shoebox on the table. "To make this official, I need some identification and one of you to sign the release form. Then, we'll be all done."

Bishop brings out his driver's license, signs the form, and we all shake hands. "One more thing." Mr. Sadler looks unsure of himself for the first time. "Your uncle left instructions for his cremated remains to be, ah, *processed* until the ashes were very fine, so we complied. I'm not quite sure what that's about but I wanted you to be aware."

I hide my surprise. "Yes, that has to do with Uncle Howard's final wishes. Thank you, Mr. Sadler. You've been very helpful." Bishop takes the box and we're escorted to the entrance. Somewhere I hear faint music and soft voices of a funeral in progress. That gives me an idea.

"Bishop, let's go visit Mom, Dad, and Knight, OK?"

to do list

- Check on Sammie
- Send Max an OSU jersey
- Imagine...
-
-
-
-
-
-
-
-

CHAPTER TWENTY-NINE

August

Memories

Crestline Cemetery is deserted.

Bishop and I walk through rows of stone markers until we reach the family plot. It's shaded by some small maples, and I'm grateful to step out of the sun.

The inscription on the left side of the large stone reads

Franklin James Brownlee
July 20, 1913 – January 14, 1999
Family Man and Chess Player

And on the right side

Elizabeth Elaine Rawlings Brownlee
September 3, 1914 – March 24, 2005
She Dwells in the House of the Lord Forever

Bishop brushes leaves from the top of our parents' head-stone. I step a few paces to my right and read the carving on the smaller stone.

Knight Rawlings Brownlee
October 12, 1945 – December 9, 2006
Beloved Son and Brother

I take a deep breath and press back the tears that sting my eyes. I miss my parents and brother. I picture us gathered around our small kitchen table eating supper on a fall evening. Dad is teasing Bishop about a girl, Knight is enjoying the food, and I'm in middle school, so I'm thinking about boys or home-work. Honestly, by the time you figure life out, it's almost over. *Why didn't I notice the beauty and love of that moment?*

I turn to find Bishop a few feet behind me and slip under his arm. He draws me close, and I hear his voice rumble in his chest. "We had good parents, Rook. We were lucky."

"You're the good guy, the rock. That last year of Knight's life…"

Bishop gives my shoulder a squeeze, walks over, and points at the ground next to Knight. "That's where Barb and I will be."

"Have you decided on an inscription?"

"I'm thinking, 'Safe in the Everlasting Arms.' Barb hasn't decided."

I see a line of aprons marching in front of me. I know the perfect inscription for Barb. *Stick a fork in her; she's done.* I suppress a smile and watch Snarky Rook high-five Witty Rook under the disapproving stare of Appropriate Rook.

Bishop continues, "I've written up notes for my service: which hymns, which scriptures. I'd be honored if you'd say a few kind words."

"Done and done." I say it lightly but feel a clench in my stomach. I don't want to think about being the only one left in my family. Nobody around to laugh about the Great Pumpkin Incident or remember my bravura performance in the fifth-grade musical.

"And you? Any ideas for a headstone inscription?"

"Oh, you know me. The Queen of the 'To Do' List. I'm picturing a big checkmark next to the word *Die*."

I stoop to pull a weed from my mother's grave. "But no headstone for me. It's cremation all the way, just like Howard. Instead of being scattered, though, Campbell and I want to find an artist to make a bronze sculpture to hold our ashes, so we can live on as an *objet d'art*."

"Useful even after death. Totally you."

"I might have to change the plan. Given the current state of our relationship, Campbell and I may want to occupy separate containers. Or maybe Jay will want his father on the mantle, but be happy to throw me out in the backyard."

"I hear bitterness. You've gone to the dark side."

"I need another sermonette, I guess." I face Bishop. "I'm thinking about the line down through the generations. Mom and Dad, the three of us, our kids, their kids. The decisions we make, the effect those decisions have."

"Here's a sermonette: Micah 6:8. *What does the Lord require of you? To act justly and to love mercy and to walk humbly with your God.*"

These instructions remind me of AA. A three-step program

instead of twelve steps. Simpler. *Harder?* You could spend a life-time working these steps.

We stand a few moments longer, silent, sunk in our private memories. I hold out my hands in front of my brother. "Tell me the truth. These look like Mom's hands, right? Veins, spots, wrinkles. We're turning into our parents, Bishop. I'm in the third quarter of my life, and I'd like to learn a few new moves."

"When the student is ready, the teacher appears, grasshopper."

We walk to the RV in silence. It's August. Back-to-school season. Time to open my mind and learn some hard lessons. *Is Dr. Canon the teacher? Bishop? Heaven forbid, Campbell?*

Dr. Canon says I absorbed the lessons my parents taught me, almost too well. My mother taught me to love reading, singing, and good cooking. She showed me, by example, what it means to support your church and community. Dad tackled the problems of life with hard work, having the right tools, and whistling. They both believed in education, prayer, and standing up for what's right.

Nothing wrong with those lessons.

But I know what Dr. Canon means. A constant drumbeat of shoulds and musts can get a person down. You have to make space for mistakes, and failure.

Take Dad's favorite pastime: chess. In chess, every game is a zero-sum game. There are clear and identifiable opponents. Every move is carefully thought out and either brings you closer to victory or to defeat. The pieces always move in the same way. I've always related to those aspects of my father's favorite pastime.

But what if chess is a bad model?

All the advice I'm hearing is about giving up control,

moving in a new way, being spontaneous. *What model is that?* Checkers? A Rubik's Cube? Twister?

Back at the RV, Bishop takes the wheel and says, "I need to go to the church and work on my real sermon. I don't think a sermonette will cut it with the Abernathys. Shall I drop you at home?"

"Sure." I turn to my brother, inspired. "Coming here to Crestline has given me an idea about Howard's request if the OSU thing doesn't work out. What do you think of this? We could hire a few horn players and a drummer and do a procession to the family plot. Have a magician who would perform some tricks, you say a few words, and we scatter the ashes next to Aunt Catherine. Presto chango! He's there, and he's not there. Appropriate, meaningful, and fun."

"Not bad. You got the band thing and the joke thing. I like it. Let's put it in the second slot. We could do it over Thanksgiving weekend. In fact, I hereby invite you and yours back here to Ohio for turkey day."

"That's a nice invite. If I still have a family at Thanksgiving."

"You cannot say stuff like that. Restate, please."

Years of doing Bishop's bidding kicks in. "Thank you for the invitation. We would love to join you for Thanksgiving, and by *we*, I mean my entire family of five."

"Better." Bishop opens a case on the floor and flips through his CD collection. "I've got Motown, Johnny Cash, the Beatles, Sinatra, The Beach Boys, Elvis, and the Stones. What'll it be? Also hymns and classical."

I'm impressed with his wide-ranging taste and choose The Beach Boys. We ride north singing about surfing and young love.

Wouldn't it be nice?

to do list

- Ask Campbell re Max
- Room in luggage for
- Howard mementos?
- THINK about ashes
-
-
-
-
-
-
-

CHAPTER THIRTY

August

Eruption

I call Campbell, hoping he won't answer.

"Hello?"

"Hi, it's me. Thought I should check in to see how you and Sammie are."

"She's fine, once I re-introduce myself to her every night. She keeps making puppy dog eyes at me, which she obviously can pull off quite well, but mostly we just go to our separate corners and co-exist, like East and West Germany." Once, as a joke, he'd put Sammie on the porch in a basket with an "Adopt Me" sign while he hid in the foyer watching for my reaction. I laughed, but he knew I was *not amused.* "I'm sure she'd rather you were here, but she'll survive. What's happening there?"

I give a brief report: the lawyer, the funeral home, Howard's final wish. Campbell doesn't ask about the inheritance, and I'm glad. I've had an idea about it that I don't want to share yet. "How's Max?"

"I stopped by yesterday after school. We played with his blocks and trucks for a while."

"Is that it?"

"What else do you want to know?"

"More. What's the mood there? When are they going to unbar the door?"

"Don't make this about you. For once, let other people come to their own conclusions without coaching them."

"Geez. Really? You're going to lecture me? You aren't the one being denied access to Max. In fact, why aren't you refusing to go there until I can go? It seems like you've taken a side. And it's not mine."

"Why do there have to be sides? We all want the same thing—for Max to recover and us to come back together as a family."

"They have a funny way of getting to togetherness, by insisting on separating us."

"They're hurting for Max, so their emotions are running high. Making sense isn't their objective right now. That may be a key goal for you, but for most people, logic gives way to feelings."

"So, I'm a cold-hearted bitch."

"Wow. Only you could turn a conversation into a fight in fifteen seconds. I didn't use that label, but since you brought it up, yeah, you are an ice queen."

"And you're Mr. Understanding. The calm, collected principal. Mellow and kind. Except we both know that's not true. At home, you can be just as nasty and mean as they come."

"I have to be, to hold my own against you."

A crack of thunder interrupts us. I turn to the window of Bishop's guest room, startled. Rain peppers the glass, as a late afternoon storm moves through central Ohio. I've been jolted out of the rhythm of the argument. Lost my place. *Is it my turn to insult Campbell or his to insult me?*

Campbell jumps in. "Never mind. Let's just end this call. Why don't you talk to your brother? Maybe you'll listen to him. You sure don't listen to me."

"Telling me to *slow my roll* doesn't help. I'm doing everything that everybody suggests. Staying away from Max. Going to therapy. Practicing Centering Prayer. Giving everything time. But I don't feel different, and things aren't improving. If anything, you and I are in a worse place than before."

"We're under a lot of stress. You're retired, or at least you're not working right now. We've moved to a new state. I have a new job. We have a new grandson. That's a lot of change. The accident was just the tipping point."

"Or it just revealed the rotten foundations. We should be able to weather some changes without collapsing. Is there any news about the lawsuit?"

"No. I think it's going to take a long time."

"Something else for me to feel bad about."

"God, Rook! Get off the pity pot. You don't have to take the blame for that lawsuit."

"But I feel like I do. It's like dropping a big rock in a pond. The ripples just keep going."

"Well, boo-hoo. Poor Rook. You know what? I hate what happened to Max and to that Hammond woman, but if there's one silver lining to this whole thing, it's that you get to be on the wrong end of the stick for once. Rook McFadden, the pillar of the community, outstanding employee, maker of lists, church elder, and so on—ad nauseam. I'm glad you got knocked off your pedestal and can join the rest of us down here in the muck of real life."

The words land between us, oozing with animosity. *So that's how he really feels.* The seconds slide by. I consider the altered landscape of my life, my marriage. I force my shoulders down. They've been hunched up around my ears. I take a deep breath and roll my neck around. Hear a few cracks. "I've got to go. Bishop and I are going through Howard's house tomorrow, and then I'm supposed to come home, but maybe it'd be better if I stayed here longer." Campbell meets that idea with silence, so I voice a last, nasty retort. "So I can wallow in the muck of real life."

"Look. I'm unhappy. You're unhappy. You're struggling, and I think the way out is just give up control. Like AA says, admit your powerlessness."

"Why don't you keep your AA advice to yourself?" I snarl out a goodbye and hang up. Campbell's advice is annoyingly close to Bishop's. *Let go. Be. Soften. Relax. Forgive.* My impulse is more along the lines of *Attack. Threaten. Punish. Plot. Control.*

I yam what I yam, and that's all what I yam.

I am—or have somehow come to be—one way, yet everyone says I need to be a different way. How do I make that happen?

Don't make it happen. That's the whole point. Don't do anything. Just let go and be. This little tie-dyed Hippie in my head rarely makes an appearance. She's dancing around in a slow circle now, swaying. Should I tell Dr. Canon about all the voices in my head? Am I a budding schizophrenic? Or are these nuggets of wisdom from my subconscious?

I sit for a half an hour going over the advice I've been given. Campbell called me an ice queen, but he's wrong. What I feel in my belly isn't ice; it's fire. A wave of boiling anger that I keep under careful control because when it erupts, it destroys everything nearby. *What's the source of all that anger?* All I can come up with is that when the world fails to conform to my expectations, it pisses me off. Royally.

I have a new project to work on. Me.

Max, the Hammonds, Campbell—they're all just proxies for the real goal: a new and improved Rook, version 2.0. The problem is I have no idea what the project steps are. What do I do first?

I'll just keep following the yellow brick road. Inspired by this reference to one of my favorite childhood books and movies, I cast myself as the heroine of the story: Dorothy. Sammie is Toto, of course. I'm a little foggy about Bishop. The Scarecrow? Dr. Canon is obviously the Wizard. Campbell?

100% Flying Monkey.

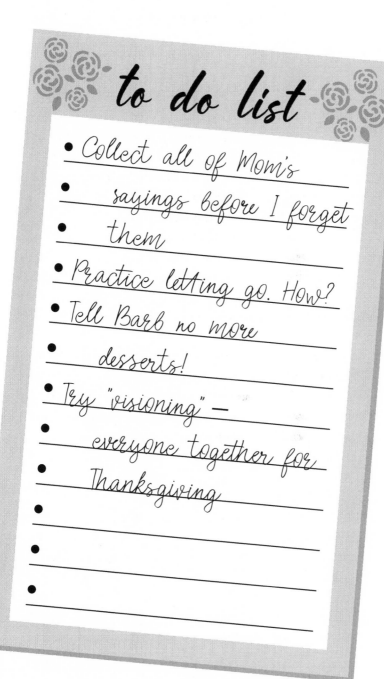

to do list

- Collect all of Mom's
- sayings before I forget
- them
- Practice letting go. How?
- Tell Barb no more
- desserts!
- Try "visioning" —
- everyone together for
- Thanksgiving
-
-
-

CHAPTER THIRTY-ONE

August

Sorting

Bishop holds up Howards' trumpet.

"How's this? We put Uncle Howard's cremains in his trumpet. Seal up the ends and voila—you have a fun and meaningful resting place. Not to mention appropriate. Good, huh?"

"That is good. Will they fit?"

"Mmm." Bishop peers into the bell of the trumpet. "Might have to ask someone in a music store how much space there is in one of these things."

Bishop puts the trumpet to his lips and blows. I recoil. "Careful. All the goats within five miles will be at the front door."

We continue our sifting and sorting in silence. I stack band coasters and tell Bishop, "I mentioned the Ohio State band to my therapist, and he had no idea what I was talking about. I figured everybody in the country knew about them. The Best Damn Band In The Land. TBDBITL. I even had to explain how to pronounce it: Ta-biddle."

"Well, believe it or not, there are people who don't care about football or marching bands at all."

"OK. Football I get. But what's not to like about marching bands? I loved being in the band in high school: the uniform, the parades, the bus rides to away football games." I tap a coffee-table book cover displaying the famous Script Ohio formation. "I want a few of these band mementos, but do you think OSU would like any of them? In fact, do you think we could get Howard mentioned at a halftime show? As a major benefactor?"

"No. That's not going to happen."

"We could ask. Let's go see some band officials, dangle all these juicy artifacts in front of them, and ask. Can't hurt."

"If we can get an appointment, I'll go with you, but they're not going to be interested in the wishes of an alumnus who graduated in 1939." Bishop points at a photo on the wall of the Goodyear Blimp poised above Ohio Stadium. "We'd have better luck getting the ashes thrown out of the blimp, which is to say, zero."

By early afternoon we've chosen our keepsakes and written up an inventory of the more interesting band artifacts. I turn to my brother. "Let's work the phones and see if there's anything else we can get done before I fly out. I'm going out on the screened porch to call the university." Bishop agrees and heads to the dining room.

I spend forty-five minutes being transferred, accidentally

disconnected, and listening to hold music, but strike gold at the end. "Hey, smarty-pants," I tell Bishop, stepping into the dining room, where he's writing in a small notebook. "I scored us an appointment with an assistant band director. He wants to hear about the memorabilia and our ideas about the scholarship money. So there. He has thirty minutes tomorrow."

Bishop sticks his tongue out. "Excellent work, Watson. Through my choir director, I found us some actual band members, and they're willing to talk in exchange for pizza. If you can delay going back to Colorado for a couple of days, we can knock this out."

"Why wouldn't I want to stay? You drive me around and give me lectures. I get to visit interesting cultural sites like lawyer's offices and funeral homes. Best. Vacation. Ever."

Bishop raises his eyebrows and pretends to write in his tiny notebook. He glances at me again, followed by more pretend note-taking.

"Who are you? Santa Claus? St. Peter? Tracking my behavior?"

"Just taking notes for a sermon. It's about being truthful rather than sarcastic."

The truth? Without Max, I'd rather be here anyway.

Bishop stops writing and throws his shoulders back. "We can try the assistant director and band members, but I think Howard may have to settle—Ha! Get it? Settle?—for a less exciting finish than he wanted."

I join Bishop at the dining room table, where I smooth and straighten the heavy Damask tablecloth. This room has been the backdrop for countless family gatherings in my life: birthdays, anniversaries, graduations, and baptisms. If I'm honest, in addition to those happy events, I've also witnessed fiery arguments, accusations, tears, and abrupt departures, proving that life is messy and relationships are complicated.

I frown at my brother. "Why do people even care where their ashes get scattered? Pretty manipulative—reaching out from the great beyond to make demands."

Bishop overlooks my pissy tone. "I imagine they enjoy putting the finishing touches to their story. Writing a proper ending." He turns to me, smiling. "Like dotting an *i*, or crossing a *t*. Or dotting *the i*."

I'm a confirmed *i* dotter, so this analogy drains away my irritation. *Huh.* Family members being unreasonable.

I can relate.

to do list

- Where's my clarinet?
- Just wondering
- Journal
- Take Calvin for a walk
- Hold it together
-
-
-
-
-
-

CHAPTER THIRTY-TWO

September

Denied

I t's Uncle Howard's "band room" on steroids.

Dr. Ward, the assistant OSU band director, is not a tidy man. His office is cluttered with posters, plaques, trophies, newspaper articles, magazine covers, and sheet music. The mass has overtaken the display shelves and started an assault on the floor itself. Rather than take the chair Dr. Ward offers at his small conference table, I wander along the walls.

"I've collected a lot of band memorabilia," he says, trailing after me.

"What's this?" I indicate a glass-topped display case.

"That's part of my baton collection. I have more at home. See, there's wood, acrylic, all kinds of handles and lengths."

"Does the baton choose you? You know, like Harry Potter's wand?"

Dr. Ward laughs. "If only they were magical. There are some trombone players I'd like to turn into toads."

I notice some sheet music on a table, and Dr. Ward says, "Our arrangers just finished those for the Penn State game. We have a unique sound, one that's unmistakably The Ohio State University Marching Band. Our in-house arrangers put that stamp on every piece we play."

I'm impressed. This band is a big business.

Bishop waves me over to see a framed T-shirt that reads

HEY FOOTBALL TEAM
GET OFF THE
BAND FIELD

We settle at Dr. Ward's table and go over the list of Uncle Howard's artifacts, then move on to the topic of the band scholarship money, our ruse for getting an appointment. We have no intention of meddling with the scholarships. Bernie's going to handle all that.

"What criteria do you have in mind?" Dr. Ward spreads his hands apart, and I almost expect him to rap one of his batons on the edge of the table. "For example, do you want the recipients to be music majors?"

"Aren't all the band members music majors?" Bishop is surprised.

"No, more than seventy percent aren't. We have earth science majors, history, math, pre-law, you name it. The university offers hundreds of majors. But, most of these kids *have* dreamed about being in the marching band since grade school."

"How many spots are open each year?" I ask.

"All of them. You have to earn your spot every year. There are two hundred and twenty-eight openings and four hundred students try out." He sits back, pleased. "You have to be top-notch and not just musically. There's also marching ability. Marching takes a lot of energy. We use a high step, and swinging those heavy horns around, moving all over the field, memorizing all the music—it's an athleticism all its own."

Dr. Ward leans forward. "These kids make a tremendous time commitment. I'd say they spend an average of twenty-five to thirty hours a week practicing, memorizing music, and being at the pre-game pep rally as well as the game. After football season, we disband, no pun intended, then form again the next year."

I probe for a way in, or I should say, *on* to the field. "Your halftime shows are spectacular. Who thinks them up? Do you ever repeat one? Are they already planned for this season?"

"Let's see. The answers are 'everyone,' 'no,' and 'yes.' Each spring we have a session and everyone pitches ideas for halftime shows: kids, directors, secretaries, the more the merrier. Then a committee picks the finalists. Over the summer, we plan each show in detail: the formations, the props, and the music."

"I have an idea for next year. Want to hear?"

"Absolutely. But the criteria are tough: It has to be about ten minutes long, the formations have to make sense from the stadium seats, and the theme should have widespread fan appeal. We also have to get the copyrights to the music."

"OK. My idea is a tribute to cartoon characters, like Road Runner, Mickey Mouse, Popeye, Bugs Bunny, etc. Easy to form their shapes."

"Not bad. I'll tuck that away."

I dip my head in a display of modesty. "Say, has anyone ever interrupted a halftime show? Run out onto the field? Some fraternity kid on a bet, something like that?"

Dr. Ward nods. "I've seen it happen once. Mix, uh, *enthusiastic* young people and alcohol, and almost anything can happen. The stadium police catch them pretty quickly, and security is much tighter now, after 9/11."

He sneaks a look at his watch. "Are there any other questions? We certainly appreciate the scholarships, and I'll give the list of band memorabilia to our staff for review."

Bishop makes a final, frontal attack: "Has anybody ever asked to be buried on the field? I know OSU alums are fanatics."

Dr. Ward isn't shocked. "There have been requests, but the university denies them. If we ever said yes, the floodgates would open. Fans, band members, football players—people do love their Buckeyes." He sits back and looks thoughtful. "You know, I bet we could open a portion of campus as a cemetery and make a fortune selling plots."

Twenty minutes later, we're on the quad. Bishop leads the way toward the parking garage. "Getting Howard's ashes onto the field is like attacking a castle where the drawbridge is up, the moat is full of alligators, and there are archers every five feet along the top with flaming arrows."

"I agree. Sorry. I thought visiting Dr. Ward was a good idea, but that was a complete bust. We've got *nada*." Students hurry past us, on their way to class, or to the library, or to meet a friend. I point out one girl. "See her sweatshirt? My sorority. You pledged, but dropped out, right?"

"Yeah. The pledging ritual was not to my taste."

"I think boys had it really different than girls. All I remember about pledging are candles, flowers, tea, some sort of origin myth, and reciting the Greek alphabet before a match burned down and out. Nothing unpleasant. But Campbell? His pledge class got beaten with wooden paddles, were forced to eat raw eggs, stay up for days, and drink ridiculous amounts of liquor."

It was the hunter-gatherer society writ small. Sororities were gatherers: circled and linked over singing, secrets, shared camaraderie. Fraternities were hunters: standing side by side, fighting other fraternities, challenging each other to outrageous dares like running naked across campus at midnight.

Uncle Howard has challenged *us* to an outrageous dare.

Which we're failing, spectacularly.

to do list

- How scatter ashes?
- Look at family albums
-    w/ Bishop & Barb
- More Enneagram
- Every day in every way
-    I'm getting — what?
-
-
-
-
-
-

CHAPTER THIRTY-THREE

September

Stricken

Bishop's scone looks twice as big as mine.

We're seated at a rickety table in a coffee shop near campus. We're here to discuss the Dr. Ward visit and hatch new plans. I've allowed myself a maple scone as a treat, yet as I eye my brother's snack, familiar childhood grievances flare. *He's got more. It's not fair.*

"Did you like having a little sister? Was I a pain?"

"Where'd that come from?" Bishop laughs. "You and Knight were both pains. It's the role of younger siblings. I loved you guys."

I roll my eyes. "Oh puh-lease. You're too good to be true. Were you always this noble? What formed your sterling personality? Nature or nurture?"

"What's got you on this track? Seeing a therapist?"

"I guess. I'm trying to figure out what makes me tick.

Birth order? Gender? DNA? Where I grew up or where I went to school? Family dynamics?"

"You were a completely normal little girl. Well, no, that's not true. You weren't. You liked playing army and cowboys more than playing with dolls. Which was OK. You made a good foot soldier in General Bishop's battalion until you got a little too mouthy and had to go."

Being with Bishop is fun and frustrating. All the patterns of our childhood are clicking back into place: the teasing, the pet names, the little jealousies. It feels like home. "So you did reject me. I knew it was something to do with you."

"We just went our separate ways. Five years is a big gap. The Brownlees were an average American working-class family. Nothing mysterious."

We both look out into the middle distance, weighing his words. "Well," he amends, "not completely average. There's Knight."

"Yes," I agree. "There's Knight."

Bishop drums his fingers on the table. "I think we're at an impasse. I didn't hear anything useful in our meeting with Dr. Ward, and those three actual band members were a complete brick wall."

"I agree. I never realized how passionate band members are. It's like the marines. Semper Fi."

The previous evening, we'd visited three members of the band, who lived together near campus. I'd been startled by the house, a once stately Victorian losing a long battle with careless and indifferent college students. Going up the broken sidewalk, I'd noticed a small tree growing in a second story gutter and shivered.

We'd bought the boys pizza: two pepperoni, sausage, and bacon monstrosities that they devoured while listening to our pitch. It went downhill from there. No, they wouldn't scatter any ashes. No, they didn't know anyone who would. No, a financial incentive wouldn't change their minds. They were too busy counting, watching, playing, and marching to fulfill our request, and they had no interest in jeopardizing their standing in the band.

Bishop pulls his legs out of the way of a girl heading to the restroom. "I was surprised to learn they don't even practice in Ohio Stadium but have a separate field for that."

I sip my tea. "I'm relieved, to tell you the truth. Trying to get people to break the rules is not my style."

My cell phone rings, and I dig it out of my purse. *Campbell.* I resent him interrupting my tea and scone. *What does he want?* I ignore it.

I refocus on Bishop, munching his bigger scone, and ask, "What do you think Howard would prefer as a lame, second-choice resting place?"

Bishop brushes crumbs from his shirt. "Howard was all about *joie de vivre.* I remember one time we had lunch together and he was excited because he'd found some trick golf balls he was going to use on his friends."

That stirs a memory. "Hey, I just thought of a Howard story. One time Mom and I stopped by Buckeye Brands to drop off some papers. I liked going there because he usually gave me some office supplies to take home. I loved all that stuff: pens, pencils, paper clips, highlighters."

"I know. He kept me in typing paper all through high school."

"Anyway, Howard was in a good mood, because he'd pulled a prank on Mike Watterson, his partner. Poor Mr. Watterson. While he was out seeing a vendor, Howard wrapped Mike's entire desk in saran wrap. I mean the whole thing: phone, adding machine, stapler, and family photos—the works."

Bishop laughs. "Never heard that one."

As the baristas shout out orders, and students scrape their chairs into constantly different configurations, I feel my equilibrium teeter. I'm bothered more by conditions in my environment—the heat, cold, smoke, light, noise—than the average person, so the noisy and stuffy coffee shop starts to get to me. I saw a statistic that said about fifteen percent of the population is highly sensitive. *Great. Another way to be an outlier.* When this happens with Campbell, he teases me, but I have to concede, he tries to accommodate my fussing whenever I'm in a draft or under a speaker or have the sun in my eyes or want the AC changed.

As my discomfort increases, I recall a recent lunch I had in a Grant Falls coffee shop when I was deep in the Enneagram book. While I read and sipped my coffee, two women came in, and I knew immediately they would be disturbing my peace. Taking their triple, venti, half-sweet, non-fat, caramel macchiatos to a nearby table, they continued their conversation in loud voices. I shot them a killer glance, but they didn't notice. The blonde, mid-story, told her friend, "THEN I SAID, YOU CAN'T TALK TO MY KID THAT WAY!"

I stopped reading. *Let's see. What coping mechanism would be best? Confrontation? Retreat? Murder?* I indulged myself with a vivid fantasy: A T-Rex appeared at the door of the café, made eye contact with me, nodded slightly, then snatched the offenders up in his huge mouth and withdrew. Their horrified screams faded.

Back in the Columbus coffee shop, I'm considering a similar fate for a couple of jocks nearby when my phone dings again. The sound that signals a text. I glance at it. It's from Campbell: CALL! IN PRIVATE. IMPORTANT!

"I guess I need to call Campbell." I take the last bite of my scone, wash it down with tea, and go stand in front of the coffee shop, the most private place I can find. I call my husband, but he doesn't answer. *Maddening.* I break my rule of never calling Campbell at school and dial his secretary, Vivian. She goes to get him out on the playground, and he's on the phone in four minutes.

"Campbell. What is it? Is it Max? Is it Sammie?" *I don't ask, "Is it you?"*

"Michelle Hammond is dead."

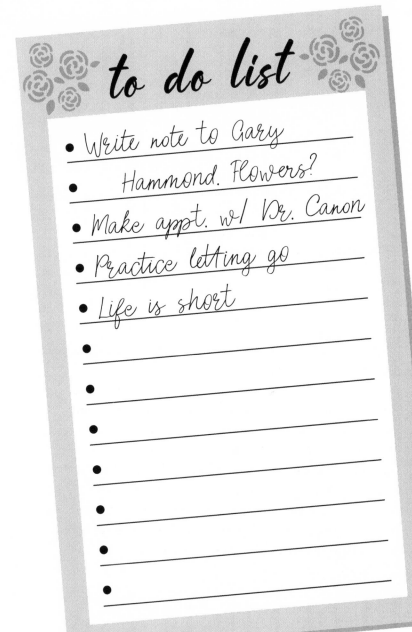

to do list

- Write note to Gary
  Hammond. Flowers?
- Make appt. w/ Dr. Canon
- Practice letting go
- Life is short
-
-
-
-
-
-
-

CHAPTER THIRTY-FOUR

September

Churning

I try to claim half the armrest from my seatmate, but my heart's not in it.

I want to take up the smallest amount of space possible. Stay out of everyone's way. Be overlooked. My thoughts are scattered and redundant. I know almost nothing about Michelle Hammond, but I can't stop thinking about her. Campbell had no information beyond the fact that her kids found her slumped in the kitchen, unconscious, so I invent facts. *She had an undiagnosed brain aneurism. She had an undiagnosed drug habit. She had an undiagnosed heart defect.*

I inspect the crumpled fax Campbell sent.

The Denver Post
September 25, 2008

BRIEFS
Lakewood Woman Dies

Lakewood resident Michelle Hammond, 33, was taken to St. Anthony's Hospital Thursday afternoon after being found unresponsive at her home. Emergency room staff pronounced her dead after extensive efforts to revive her proved unsuccessful. The married mother of two sustained a serious head injury in a July car accident. Funeral arrangements are pending.

I take out the plain notecard and envelope I borrowed from Barb and write.

September 26, 2008
Dear Mr. Hammond,

I was so sorry to read about Michelle in the *Post*. I can't imagine the pain you're going through. Please know that you and your children have my deepest sympathy, and I'll be thinking of you in the days to come.

Sincerely,
Rook McFadden

I reread it a dozen times. *What tripe.* I crumple it up and stuff it in the seatback pocket in front of me. Gary Hammond doesn't want my sympathy. He wants my heart on a spit. All the good feelings I enjoyed in Columbus are gone. *Two steps forward and three steps back.* Guilt washes over me. That poor man. Those poor children.

The Enneagram says that Type Ones, "Reformers" like me, believe they have to be perfect to be loved and must be right to be perfect. It was horrible enough before, with Max and Michelle injured. Now, Michelle is dead, and my mind darts about, searching for an escape. How can I bear this additional weight? I miss Bishop already, listening patiently, helping me sort through the drama and wrong conclusions.

I close my eyes and picture the Hammond house. No one is in the front yard, and I walk with confidence to the door and ring the bell. Michelle answers. She's alone. Soon we're sharing tea and muffins while I look through a photo album on the coffee table.

"These muffins are wonderful," Michelle says. "I'm not as good a cook now. Sometimes the recipes confuse me, or I forget if I've added the salt already and do it again." She giggles at her ineptitude.

Ashley and her brother burst into the room, toss their backpacks on the couch, and crowd around their mother. I can tell Ashley's senses are on high alert. I catch the suspicious looks and know this seven-year-old is the protective lioness in the room, Michelle the cub. A reversal of the normal order. It reminds me of my relationship with Knight. The boy gobbles down a muffin and is out the door to the backyard within three minutes. I ask Michelle, "Are you in any pain from the accident?"

"I take some pain meds and some stuff for when I get anxious." She points at her head and makes a face, "It's a bit scrambled in there, but I have my good girl Ashley, Gary, my mom, friends, and neighbors—lots of people helping out."

As I leave, I offer help with meals, but Michelle waves me off. At the door, she looks upset for the first time. "Did I cause the accident? I don't remember, but if it's true, I'm so sorry. Please forgive me."

I grab both of Michelle's hands and lean close. "I don't think anybody knows exactly what happened out there. Let's just agree to forgive each other, OK?" Michelle nods, and Ashley, peeking out from behind her mother, gives me an unguarded and approving smile.

The pilot's voice over the loudspeaker breaks into my daydream. "We're making our final approach into Denver. We should be at the gate in about fifteen minutes. Please turn off all electronic devices. Please return your seatbacks and tray tables to their full, upright position."

Please turn off your fantasies and return your mind to its full, uptight position.

I comply with the pilot's requests and spend the final minutes of the flight deciding what version of Rook will step off the plane. I'm some strange mixture of sad, resigned, suspicious, and defeated.

When I was twelve, the retailers in our town sponsored a Halloween soap drawing contest. If you entered, you could draw on the big glass windows of the stores along Main Street. These Halloween-themed sketches were admired by shoppers, photographed for the local paper, judged, and awarded prizes by the merchants. My mother entered me in the contest and came up with a sketch and poem. I did the drawing and printing, and to our delight, I won in my category.

Our entry depicted two witches—one ugly and one beautiful— much like the stock characters from the Walt Disney classics or *The Wizard of Oz*. The accompanying poem asked

If you were a witch,
Which witch would you be?
A witch like I am?
Or a witch like me?

Arrows led from words to figures. I've long forgotten the prize—I think maybe it was $5—but the words have stuck in my memory all these years.

I don't want to be a witch at all.
Do I get a choice?

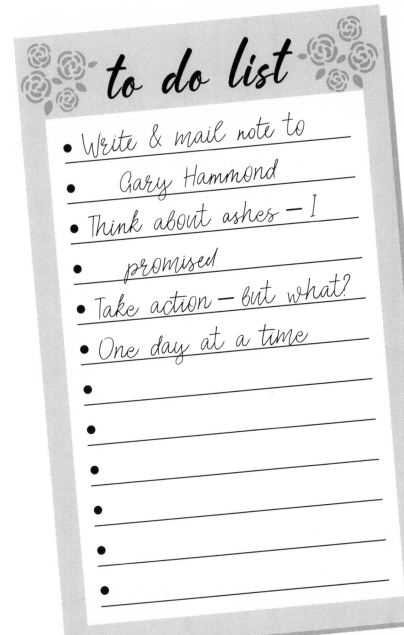

to do list

- Write & mail note to
- Gary Hammond
- Think about ashes — I
- promised
- Take action — but what?
- One day at a time
-
-
-
-
-
-

CHAPTER THIRTY-FIVE

September

Loggerheads

The fight starts on the trail.

"Michelle's death. That was a shocker." Campbell looks up from his breakfast on Saturday morning. "Do you think it will have any impact on the lawsuit?"

"If it's linked to the accident, I imagine it means Gary will ask for more money. And he should. He's going to need it, with two kids to raise alone."

Campbell takes his plate to the sink. "Poor guy."

I picture Gary making breakfast for his two children this morning. Their tears. Their sadness and confusion. I send a little prayer down to Lakewood.

Campbell starts for the garage, then turns back. "Hey, what if I skipped my meeting this morning and we went for a hike at Three Sisters? Might feel good to get out and walk."

Named for a rock formation, Three Sisters Park is near the house and features several good trails. I nod and assemble our usual hiking snack: a thermos of coffee and two raisin bran muffins, which I allow on my approved snack list.

Thirty minutes later, we're on one of the trails, which leads into deep woods. It's cool and quiet, with only the crunch of our boots to interrupt the birdsong and squirrels' chatter. Campbell, ahead of me, breaks the mood. "I've been thinking about the money from Howard's house and what to do with it. Want to hear?"

I don't. "Sure."

"First, give away ten percent."

I nod at his back in approval.

"Next I think we should set up a savings account for Max for college. Pay some on the mortgage. Then take a great vacation. What are you thinking?

I navigate the trail, stomach clenched, knowing I'm about to poke the bear. "You're not going to like what I'm thinking. I want to give some money to the Hammonds. Now, wait, wait. Before you melt down, just listen. OK?"

He does not wait. Stops walking. Turns. "Are you kidding? You can't be serious! That's, that's…" His voice gets louder. "That's insane. Give it to the Hammonds?"

"Not all of it. Just enough to make a difference. We could set up—"

"No." His interruption, tone, and fierce look throw me off my game.

"I've talked to Howard's lawyer about setting up an annuity. That way Gary could hire some help, or…"

"How much?"

"$25,000?" I deliver it as a question. A rookie mistake.

"$25,000?" He explodes. I glance behind me, concerned that the couple thirty yards back will call a park ranger or pull out their pepper spray. I push Campbell off the trail and smile as they edge past. "Hi, there. Great day, isn't it?" I find a log a little way into the woods and sit down. Campbell selects a large rock with a flat top and sits facing me.

"Rook, you don't owe that family anything. It's tragic about Michelle, but giving money to the Hammonds? You're crazy, and I can't believe we're even having this conversation. They're suing us, for heaven's sake." He pulls the thermos from his backpack and pours himself a cup of coffee.

I shift on the log. Consider how to advance my argument. "I know Michelle wasn't wearing her seat belt, but remember all the times you drove drunk? What if you'd hit someone, hurt someone? You made terrible choices. Drank, took drugs. And here you are today—respectable, healthy, not a scratch. Yet, Michelle, the mother of two, forgets a seat belt and pays the ultimate price. Where's the justice? It's just a way to thank the universe for our good fortune."

"Seriously? You're bringing that up? I'm grateful every day that I never had an accident when I was drinking. I've made amends. I do good work at school. I'm a good husband, father, and grandfather. I support my church, and I go to AA." Campbell's list is accurate, but he's missing the point.

I plunge ahead. "I stayed with you through all those bad years. All that shit. Supported, loved, and forgave you. Now I'm asking for the same thing from you."

Campbell's face is a storm cloud. "You want to rehash stuff that happened thirty years ago?"

"No, I just need to do something. AA says to take action. I thought this plan was a way to take action." A squirrel runs up the trunk of a nearby pine and sits on a branch, chittering. I remember to breathe. Consciously lower my volume. "I can't defend it. It just feels right."

Campbell is trying to shake his head and drink coffee at the same time, which doesn't work. I do the laundry, so the stain now spreading on his hiking shirt will be mine to get out. "A guy at AA the other day used a phrase I liked: 'Not my circus, not my monkey.' But damn it, Rook, this *is* my circus. My family, my future. What if a year from now we have a health crisis? Our investments go to shit? The kids get in trouble and need help? Max needs an operation? We'd want that money and it'd be gone."

"Could I have some of that coffee?" He pours and hands me a cup. "And a muffin?" I let the quiet of the woods envelop me. Watch some ants carry off muffin crumbs. "Will you at least consider it?"

Campbell throws the last of his coffee into the pine needles. "I know you feel lousy about the Hammond family. But think about it. If the situation were reversed, I bet the Hammonds would not be writing us a check." He leans forward. "Picture this. You drive by the Hammonds a year from now and there's a new boat in the drive. Or you hear that Gary goes to the casino in Black Hawk on weekends and loses money on the slots." Campbell takes up some sticks and snaps them in two. "Or here's one, he blows it all on a pyramid scheme selling vitamins."

"Yes. I agree. He could use the money in foolish ways. So?"

"Rook, I need to protect you from doing this. They say no major decisions while you're grieving. You'll regret it."

I look at my husband. *What did I ever see in him?* A list of things I don't like about him forms in my head. The way he sneezes, the way he interrupts me, the way he can't remember the garage door code—these are just the top three.

What a jerk.

By dinnertime, we aren't talking at all. Cold silence. Heavily shut doors. Retreating to opposite ends of the house. Finally, around 8 p.m., I find him polishing his shoes. "Look, we're not getting anywhere. If you don't like my idea, then you come up with something to help the Hammonds. Propose an alternative. Or if you don't want to do that, let's get a neutral third party to arbitrate, like Rev. Leatherman or Dr. Canon."

"No." He jabs polish on his loafers "No third parties. No coming up with alternatives. Look, Howard left the money to you, not me, so I guess you get to decide what to do with it, but I'd like to think I get a vote. My vote is no money to the Hammonds."

Resigned to spending my night alone, I go to my desk and compose a short note to Gary Hammond, address and stamp the envelope, and walk it up to our mailbox, where I raise the metal flag. I leave off my personalized return address sticker. Maybe Gary will open and read it before tossing it in the trash.

I decide to work on my needlepoint. I unpack the materials and instructions for Max's stocking. It's detailed work that requires focus, and I proceed slowly, making frequent references to the pattern and instructions, inspecting the photo of the finished stocking, looking up stitches, counting, and comparing colors.

My needle comes unthreaded, and it drops to the floor.

After spending several minutes on the floor finding it, I sit back down and rethread it, only to realize I've been using the wrong stitch. Frustrated, I tear out the work I've done and drop my needle, again. "Patience, Rook," I tell myself, teeth clenched. *Another lesson from my time doing needlepoint.*

Everything I Know I Learned From Needlepoint

1. Have the right supplies and tools
2. Ask for help when you're stuck
3. When you start making multiple mistakes, stop
4. Be relaxed, neither too tight nor too loose
5. Don't get lost in the details and forget the big picture
6. Small, isolated errors won't be noticed

The next day at breakfast, Campbell and I are still giving each other the silent treatment. I watch the familiar battle play out: Good Rook, loving and church-going Rook, wants to apologize, or at least clear the air, but hurt Rook, misunderstood and stubborn Rook, is not having it. Campbell, shoveling in his oatmeal, isn't going to make the first move either. A classic stand-off. The only one unaffected by the tension is Sammie, who's taken up residence on the floor between my feet and is demolishing a stuffed toy mouse.

Fifteen minutes later, Campbell makes it clear that we won't be going to church together this morning. He pauses in the kitchen on his way out. "I hope you have a good morning." His words are stiff and dry.

"Thank you." This comes out prim and clipped.

I hear the garage door descending, like a stage curtain coming down at intermission. The midpoint of *The McFadden Marriage*: a play in two acts.

The question is, is it a comedy or a tragedy?

to do list

- Ashes ideas
- Call Jay
- Plan meals, clean house,
  - do laundry
  - OR
- Go somewhere quiet to
  - think

CHAPTER THIRTY-SIX

September

Grief

The inscriptions are heartbreaking.

The Columbine Memorial has a circular design, with the inner ring containing large table-height slabs of stone, tilted toward the visitor, engraved with the messages that the families have composed about their lost loved ones.

It doesn't take a professional like Dr. Canon to understand why I've come here.

Death. Loss. How did others cope?

The infamous high school is bordered by a large public park with acres of baseball and soccer fields, tennis courts, batting cages, playgrounds, and covered picnic tables. There's also a sizable reservoir, a skate park, walking trails, and now, a memorial, carved into the side of a hill, honoring the twelve students and one teacher killed on April 20, 1999.

The concrete path to the memorial is steep and curved and leads me into a protected earthen bowl where I can't see anything except grass-covered hills, the memorial, and the sky. I start on one end and move from one stone slab to another, reading the heartbreaking words.

"A joy."

"Always laughing."

"Kind."

"An inspiration."

Imagine writing one or two paragraphs summing up your child's life.

I suck in my breath as I read the next inscription. It's different. Jarring. This father has made a political statement linking godless schools and abortion to the Columbine murders perpetrated by Harris and Klebold. His bitter sentiment is literally carved in stone.

A man is working his way toward me. We nod, silently, as in church. He stops and says, "It feels like Columbine was the first leg of the stool to be kicked out from under us, and 9/11 was the second. Now we're just teetering. Waiting."

I consider this. *He's right, yet...*

"I'm struck by the impact a person can have, even if they live only a short time," I say. "Most of these kids were fifteen? Sixteen? They'd written poems, made career choices, helped their families, made a difference. We shouldn't give up hope." The man makes no reply, just walks on, murmuring.

I return to the inscriptions. These kids set out on a typical day, and the unimaginable happened. *Like Michelle.* A selfish thought intrudes: Max did not die on that highway. Max will heal. I grab the edge of the stone table, swaying, struck by the randomness of it all. So little we can do. *So much we can do.*

I've been on this earth sixty-two years. Plenty of time to have an impact. What would my two-paragraph inscription say?

I finish my reading, giving each child and the one adult my full, reverent consideration. I sit on a stone bench, listening to the fountain, the breeze, my breath. I dial Jay.

"Hi, Mom."

At least he picked up.

"Hi. I just wanted to hear your voice. How are you? How's Carly? And of course, Max?"

He lets the silence stretch out. When he answers, his studied, neutral tone—like he's giving a report at a staff meeting—tells me volumes. "A bit better. Max should get his wires off next week. We've been play-acting the accident with his cars and stuffed animals. His psychologist suggested that."

A two-year-old shouldn't have a psychologist. He should be having playdates, not counseling sessions. My wound opens. Seeps poison.

"I hope it helps. Uncle Bishop and Aunt Barb say hello. They send their prayers."

"How was Ohio?" I picture him watching the clock on his desk. Deciding how much time to give me. Three minutes? Four?

"A mixture. I'm going back next week to scatter Uncle Howard's ashes." I survey the conversational ground in front of me, littered with land mines. *Where to step?*

"He was a great guy. He really seemed to understand kids, so it was sad he didn't have any."

I visualize the small headstone near my parents' and Knight's graves. Howard and Catherine's son, Christopher, who died at age two of leukemia. Max's age. I remember Bishop's theological take: no family reunions in heaven. *Here, now, do what you can.* That advice seems vaguely familiar, but I can't place it.

"Jay. How are we going to fix this? I'm so distressed. I'll never drive Max again if that's what you want. Just let me back into his life, your life."

Seconds tick by. A plane, heading west, leaves a faint contrail. A hawk circles, searching for mice, rabbits, prairie dogs. Jay's voice is softer, but not tentative, as he tells me, "I'm having trouble getting over it, Mom. I've always admired you: your intellect, your common sense, your high ideals. It's hard to let that go."

Let that go? What's he saying?

Three-year-old Jay and I sing the alphabet song and draw letters on a pad of paper. Five-year-old Jay and I read *Charlotte's Web* and cry together in the armchair by the fire. Nine-year-old Jay and I wrap his gift for Father's Day and giggle over the homemade card. Sixteen-year-old Jay glares as I take away his car keys for some infraction. Eighteen-year-old Jay hugs me when he opens the early acceptance letter from Cornell, the college of his choice.

That boy, this man, now a father himself, whom I cherish, is telling me that my portrait no longer hangs in his Hall of Heroes.

I flash back, seeing the broken windshield as I dangle suspended inside my car, Max's screams fading to an eerie silence. My life got smashed that day, but Jay has just handed me a clue, like a corner piece to a 1000-piece puzzle. His words, and the pain buried inside them, reverberate in my head.

I've always admired you…. It's hard to let that go. It's not

214

just that Jay is angry with me for hurting Max. He's also angry with me for hurting him. For not living up to the perfect image I've constructed and fed him, like snake oil elixir, all these years. Turns out his mother is fallible, human, and often, just plain wrong.

"Let's just take a step toward each other, OK?" His silence creates a void I rush to fill. "Did you get the Brutus Buckeye doll I sent Max?"

"Yes. He likes it. Hey, I gotta go. Take care, Mom. Bye."

I put away my phone and sit another fifteen minutes in the sunshine. Still. Eyes closed. I push out stray thoughts and let my Centering Prayer word expand and pulse in rhythm with my breath. *Grace.*

On this hilltop, near the site of an unspeakable tragedy, I wait.

to do list

- Snuggle with Sammie
- Send Bishop & Barb a
-    thank you card
- Start college fund for
-    Max
- Standing on the promises
-
-
-
-
-
-

CHAPTER THIRTY-SEVEN

September

Break

Campbell ruins breakfast.

We're sitting at the kitchen table, nursing our hurts, when he asks, "Are you going to continue seeing Dr. Canon?"

"Why? Are you worried about the cost?"

"No. Although it does cost a shitload. Just wondering."

"Are you saying it isn't helping?"

"God, Rook. It was just a question. If you want to keep going, then go."

"I'll pay for it myself, out of my inheritance from Uncle Howard."

"Oh great. Another way to fritter away that money."

I stare at him. Close my eyes and shake my head. "Stop. Being. An. Ass." Long pauses between each word.

"Well, you're being unreasonable. We make financial decisions together, remember? You are behaving like… You're not…"

I give him a withering smile. "If you'd finish one of those sentences, we might be able to continue this conversation." I watch Campbell seethe and struggle for the right come-back. A flicker of satisfaction rises up, rewarding my meanness. I savor it, knowing I only have a moment before I reap the whirlwind.

He pushes away his plate and slams his hand on the tabletop. I jump, and Sammie barks. "God! You are impossible. I start every conversation determined to be supportive, and within two minutes, you manage to twist everything into …you twist my words …Shit!" He jumps up and stomps to the sink.

I go quiet, picking over the exchange, searching for the place it went off the rails. My silence gives Campbell space to continue his tirade.

"What do you want, Rook? Do you want me to leave you alone? Do you want me to leave permanently? I'm not a mind reader."

What I want is for Campbell to know what I want, but deep down, I understand that is not, and never has been, the dynamic between us. We chose each other because our strengths, weaknesses, needs, and abilities fit together in some strange, wonderful, effective combination. Yin and yang. Or co-dependence. Pick your label. It works, or it used to.

I stay silent for too long. I've read that introverts, like me, should be given the courtesy of the *Seven Second* rule in a conversation. Before jumping in and stepping all over our reply, give us seven seconds to respond. Campbell hasn't read that article and takes the verbal reins again.

"I'm tired of … ." He waves his arms, sweeping up our marriage, relationship, and lives in an encompassing gesture. " …this whole mess. Something needs to change."

I find my voice. "You mean *I* have to change."

"Yeah, I do mean that. I wish I had a movie of our interactions. There isn't a therapist in the world who wouldn't nail you about your destructive behaviors, and snarky-ass comments, including your precious Dr. Canon."

"All those therapists would also point out your classic gaslighting techniques: make your wife thinks she's crazy, and in the wrong." I'm not sure that makes sense, but the words are flowing and I don't care. "Why can't you be on my side? You have your job, and new colleagues, and your AA meetings, and I've got none of that. I don't have friends, or Jay, or Bishop, or anyone, really. I've got you, and you've made it very clear that I'm a burden. You think I'm emotional and needy, and behaving irrationally."

Campbell holds up his hands and cranks the handle of an imaginary movie camera. ""Exhibit A, Dr. Canon. Rook McFadden being emotional, needy, and behaving irrationally."

I jump up, knocking over my chair. Sammie squeaks and runs. "Don't worry about having to leave. I'll solve that problem. After my therapy tomorrow, I'm going back to Ohio. Bishop and I have a task to finish."

"Fine. Go, and stay as long as you want." There's steel in his voice.

"While I'm gone, why don't you go to a few AA meetings and work on your shitty behavior?"

"See, that's a perfect example of what I mean. Making it all my fault, and never taking any blame. I want to be your friend, but you are one prickly human being, you know? You scare everybody away. So go on, keep riding your high horse. I *will* go to AA, because at AA, everyone knows they're at a meeting because they screwed up, they're powerless over their addiction, and their life has become unmanageable. How's your life lately, Rook? Manageable?" After this long speech, Campbell turns away and goes out to the garage.

I sit at the table for a long time, parsing his words. My gut reaction is to label each part TRUE or FALSE.

I make everything his fault. TRUE? (*I can't help it that he's at fault a lot of the time*)

I never take any blame. FALSE (*Visit my head for proof*)

He wants to be my friend. TRUE? (*Then start acting like it, mister*)

I'm a prickly human. TRUE (*No argument there*)

I scare everybody away. TRUE? (*That hurts*)

I ride a high horse. TRUE? (*If true, that explains why I scare everybody away*)

Everyone at AA admits their powerlessness. TRUE (*That's real courage*)

I should emulate that behavior. TRUE (*And I know what Step One says to do*)

I'm discomforted to find that much of what Campbell said is valid. Now what? I look down from my high horse to the ground and tremble.

It's a long way to fall.

to do list

- Ashes ideas?
- Tell Dr. Canon to go to
-    hell
- Find Cs AA books & read
-    the steps

CHAPTER THIRTY-EIGHT

October

Useless

I s this a yoga pose?

I lie down on the couch in Dr. Canon's office and fold my hands over my stomach. This is my preferred sleep position. I'm a quiet sleeper. *If only I could quiet my mind.*

"How do you feel about Michelle Hammond's death?" Dr. Canon wastes no time.

"Wretched. Guilty. I don't know whether she took too many of the wrong pills deliberately or accidentally, but I do know it started with the car accident. I'm part of that equation."

"What would your father say about it?"

I'm shocked by the question. "My father? I don't get what you…"

"Don't overthink it. Just answer. What would he say?"

"That people have to tough it out. Handle their obligations."

"And your mother?"

"She'd have baked them a coffee cake and invited Gary and the kids to church."

"Where do you fall in that continuum of reactions?"

"Gosh, I…" I'm clenching my hands so tightly that my nails, short as they are, dig into my palms. "I'm making them sound like clichés. Hard-boiled dad and soft-hearted mom. People are more complicated than that."

"Are you more complicated than that?"

"Yes. I like to think I'm very nuanced, although the Enneagram says my go-to emotion is anger." Dr. Canon's not a fan of the Enneagram. Whenever I mention it, the temperature in the room goes down several degrees.

"You do look angry." Dr. Canon says. "What's that anger about?"

"It's about Michelle. About Campbell. About life being unfair. About paying someone to ask me questions, when being asked questions is what Campbell does that drives me crazy."

Dr. Canon makes a puffing sound. "Don't play games, Rook. You're too smart for that."

I look around for Ziggy, but he's AWOL. *His Spidey sense telling him to avoid this crazy and angry lady.*

"OK. No games." I sigh, weary of exploring my motives and feelings, but not willing to waste the money I'm spending to unburden myself.

"Tell me more about your parents."

"I told you. My dad was strict, detailed. A rules guy. My mother was fun, creative, messy. In their case, I guess opposites did attract. She was nuts about him."

"How did their relationship play out day-to-day?"

"Uh, we all tried to please him. Not upset him. Like he was simmering. Don't add fuel, if you know what I mean, or he might boil over. I was good at that—not setting him off. I knew the rules. My stupid brother, on the other hand."

"What? What did your brother do?"

"Bishop was older and should have known better. I'd watch him blunder into easily avoidable confrontations. Maybe it was a gender thing. For example, he'd borrow one of Dad's tools and then leave it out. Dumb."

"So you learned to follow the rules, or your parent would withdraw love and support."

"Well duh, isn't that every kid's experience?"

"Is it? Every kid's experience?"

"God, you are a pain in the ass. So my father liked things put away. Liked things tidy. Does that make him a bad parent? What's wrong with order? Discipline?"

"*Is* there something wrong with order or discipline?"

I fling myself up from the couch and stomp to the window. The usual Colorado sunshine. I'm furious. "Why are we talking about my father? I'm here to talk about me. About Campbell, Michelle Hammond, Jay, and people who are currently…" I almost say "alive" and realize my mistake. Michelle. *Not alive.*

Forty-five useless minutes later, I'm driving to the airport. *Getaway. Days without Dr. Canon or Campbell. Bossy men who think they know best.*

I fantasize about life without Campbell. Life as a quiet, reserved widow. During the day, I'll do my needlework, read, shop, go to the movies, or for coffee with friends. I'll have

Sammie, or some version of her, church activities, and just maybe, visits with Jay, Carly, and Max.

Nights would be tough. I see myself in an armchair as the minutes tick by. Reading, a little TV, some computer time, getting my cereal bowl and spoon out ready for breakfast. *Pathetic.* I mentally pick up my future self like a doll and set myself down in a retirement home, everyone gathered in the common area to play cards or put puzzles together. Idle chatter. Repeating everything for the hard of hearing. Some old duffer telling the same story for the zillionth time. *Ugh. No thanks.*

Would I remarry? I'm not sure. I conjure up a widower who likes museums, art house movies, and cooking gourmet meals. One who doesn't talk too much and dotes on Max. No children himself. A healthy pension. Full head of hair. Slim. Appreciates a joke. Likes to take walks. A churchgoer. Not addicted to sports on TV. No bad habits.

My merry widower and I skip off into the sunset. Dr. Canon is standing by the side of the road, frowning, tapping his right index finger against his temple. It seems I'm not permitted a fantasy life, or he's telling me to *interpret it.*

I shove my pretend husband into a ditch.

Trudge down the road by myself.

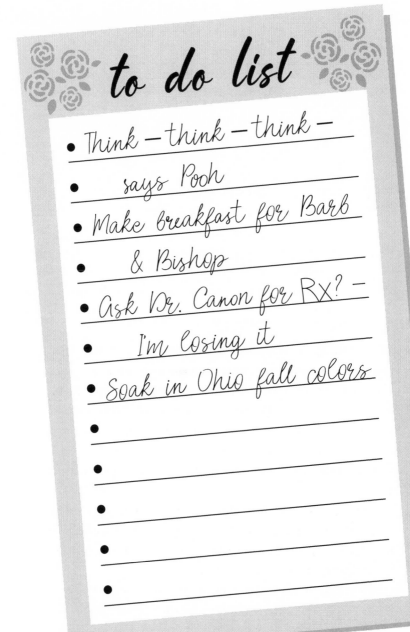

to do list

- Think — think — think —
- says Pooh
- Make breakfast for Barb
- & Bishop
- Ask Dr. Canon for Rx? —
- I'm losing it
- Soak in Ohio fall colors
-
-
-
-
-

CHAPTER THIRTY-NINE

October

Signals

T he stadium tour is worth every penny.

Bishop and I meet our stadium tour guide, Tim Cassenetta, at the main entrance in the huge north rotunda. Ohio Stadium, we learn, opened in 1922 and sits on fourteen acres. The Shoe originally held 66,000 seats in a horseshoe-shaped structure, but over the years and through various additions, it now accommodates 104,000 fans on game day.

The next stop is the Steinbrenner Band Center. Display cases hold uniforms, music, instruments. "This must have been Howard's favorite place on earth," I tell Bishop. "I bet he read every label and inscription."

We step into the cavernous practice room, where I imagine two hundred twenty-eight students playing brass and percussion instruments. *Deafening*. Chairs, music stands, and boxes are stacked in the corners. A huge mural of the band forming Script Ohio takes up the entire back wall. I cast about for a sign, a clue, a hook to help us in our mission, but nothing clicks.

"Why is it a band *director*, but a symphony *conductor*?" I ask. "They're doing the same thing, but it sounds odd to switch it: a band conductor and a symphony director." The men, deep in conversation and already moving on to the next stop on the tour, don't hear me. I trail after them, reluctant to leave the Band Center.

Usually, I'm a tour guide's dream client, listening with rapt attention, nodding in appreciation, and asking thoughtful questions. I stay near the front of tour groups, so I can catch every word. I favor the front seats in classrooms, too. Teacher's Pet? I like to think I'm just eager to learn, which is true, but it also has something to do with getting my money's worth, coupled with my poor eyesight.

"We average the highest number of total attendees at a college football game in the country, and the highest number of student attendees," Tim continues. We learn that the OSU Band Center has its own mini-cafeteria, lockers, seamstress, and trainer. "They get injured, too," Tim tells us.

We walk onto the field and stand in the middle of the **O** that is itself in the middle of the fifty-yard line. We examine the grass and sit on the team benches. The goalpost crossbar looks ridiculously narrow from this vantage point, and kicking a football between them impossible. Tim says seven to ten weddings take place each year in the end zone. "If you've got the money, you can rent almost any part of this place."

Bishop asks about security. "We have everything," Tim says. "Campus security, local police, sheriff deputies, rent-a-cops, and about a hundred homeland security people for home games. They do a bomb sweep, look under cars. We're pretty buttoned up." Bishop, standing behind Tim, mouths, "We're screwed," makes his hand into a pistol and shoots himself in the head. I bite my lip to choke back a laugh and turn away, pretending to be fascinated with the design of a nearby handrail.

We stand at the top of an escalator and look out to the west, where the Olentangy River snakes by. "Since we're in the flight path of planes coming out of Columbus International, they even divert the planes around us during a home game," Tim says. "That's true for the Goodyear Blimp and the planes pulling banners as well."

I inquire about security near the field.

"It's tight. Since they lowered the field fifteen feet in 1998, to get in more seats, it's harder to get to the field from the stands. It's crowded down there, and you have to have proper credentials." Tim looks at us sharply. "A kid ran out onto the field last year, but one of the coaches tackled him. Almost lost his scholarship."

Our tour runs another twenty minutes. We visit the press box, some suites, and the tunnel through which the football players run to make their grand entrance. By the end, I'm disheartened. I can't see how to pull this off. We walk with Tim to the entrance in the gloomy space beneath the seats, a large area crowded with vehicles, trailers, and pallets of supplies, crisscrossed by staircases and locked security gates.

I lag behind Bishop and Tim, who are engaged in an

animated conversation about the current football season. I notice a truck half hidden by a pile of hoses. I stop, duck my head, and squint. It stirs a memory. I can only see a bit of lettering on its side, and given my poor eyesight, even that is blurry. I'm maneuvering to see more when I hear Bishop calling. I walk to where the two men wait. Bishop thanks Tim and tries to give him a tip, but he refuses.

In the car, Bishop sums up the tour. "Interesting, but it convinced me we can't get Howard out there. Time to give up." He grins as inspiration strikes. "It's *Ashes Impossible.*"

"Yeah. Howard may have named his company after the Buckeyes, but that's as close as he's…" Something clicks in my brain. "Hey. I think I just saw a Buckeye Brands truck parked at the stadium. Do they do business with OSU?"

"Don't know. Seems reasonable. Why?"

"Just seems like a strange coincidence to see that truck there. What if it's a sign?"

"A sign?"

"A sign that we ought to go visit Buckeye Brands. Could we?"

Bishop works his mouth. He's given as much time as he wants to our escapade. He's got appointments. Meetings. Sermons.

"Puh-lease?"

"OK. One last effort. Then I need to get back to real life. And so do you."

What if I don't want to go back?

to do list

- Get Jay OSU sweatshirt
- Get Sammie OSU collar
- Try "I like Campbell" list
- again
- Let my light shine

CHAPTER FORTY

October

Brainstorm

"Who runs Buckeye Brands now?"

I settle into the passenger seat of Bishop's sedan, glad for the comfort but missing the bird's-eye view the RV affords. "One of the Watterson kids? There were three of them, right?"

"Yeah. Kelsey is president and Phil runs operations. Mike Jr. moved to Arizona and is a financial planner or a tax guy or something like that. I told Kelsey I'm putting together a golf tournament in honor of Howard—a fundraiser for his Rotary Club, and I'd like Buckeye Brands to be a sponsor."

"Have you always been able to lie so convincingly?" I look at Bishop with mixed admiration and disapproval.

"It's not a lie; I'm really organizing a golf tournament."

When Bishop parks in front of Buckeye Brands, I see

that it's the same nondescript low-slung building butted up against a large warehouse that I remember from long-ago visits. "Hasn't changed much," I say. "It's impressive, really, that the company Howard started over sixty years ago is still going strong."

"I think it's quite successful. I see the trucks around town, and the occasional billboard and newspaper ad."

Soon we're seated in Phil Watterson's office, which I dimly recall used to be his father's. There's new carpeting, the desk has been replaced, and the computer and phone equipment are current. I can't help but smile as I picture the original furniture encased in layers of plastic wrap. We learn that Kelsey is out of town at a conference and chat for a while about the old days, the original partners, and the longevity of the company. Bishop goes into his pitch about the golf sponsorship.

"Hey, excuse me, gentlemen. I'm going to the restroom," I say, and slip into the hall. I find the ladies' room, but just beyond it, I see the door leading to the warehouse proper. I push the door open. Immediately, sounds pull me back into my childhood: forklifts beep, large garage doors roll open and shut, voices echo from the concrete walls. I walk down rows stacked high with wooden pallets full of product, inhaling the mixture of gas, grease, paint, plastic, and ammonia that hasn't changed in fifty years. From the loading dock, I hear a radio playing and truck motors idling.

I turn a corner, see the door to a small office standing open, and peek in. There's a man seated behind a scuffed desk, drinking coffee, reading from a stack of paper, and adding an occasional mark. I look at the nameplate facing me and grin. "Walt?" I go in, extending my hand as he looks up. "It's Rook McFadden. Well, Rook Brownlee is how you knew me. Howard's niece."

The man unfolds his lanky frame and comes around the desk to grab my hand. "Rook! Of course. This is a nice surprise. What are you doing here?" We lean back and appraise each other, each making silent observations about how the other has aged.

"I can't believe you still work here. When did I last see you? I think it might have been at Uncle Howard's retirement party. Are you ever going to retire?"

Walt motions me to sit and goes back behind his desk. "I'm going to retire next January. Can you believe that'll make forty-five years I've worked here?" He looks at me with raw emotion. "I was so sad about your uncle passing. He meant the world to me. I planned on attending his memorial service, maybe even say a few words, but Kelsey told me there wasn't going to be one."

"I know. I agree with you, but Howard had other ideas. That's actually why I'm in Columbus. My brother Bishop and I are charged with scattering his ashes. But, forty-five years—what a record! Nobody does that anymore."

Walt leans back with a smile. "Thanks. I've loved working here. If you'd told my younger self that I'd someday be the manager of a fine facility like this…" He throws his arms wide to indicate the bustling warehouse. "I'd have said you were crazy. And there's only one man who made all that possible, and that man was your uncle."

"Did he hire you?"

"He did. But there's more to it than that. Don't you know

my story?" Walt looks surprised, then bobs his head in sudden understanding. "Of course. Howard was just protecting my privacy. Let me tell you how I came to Buckeye Brands, and you'll appreciate what a special man he was. This is what I would have said at the memorial service anyway." I sit back, pleased to hear a new story about Howard.

"When I was eighteen, I got in trouble—breaking and entering. I went to prison for three years, and when I got out, my prospects were pretty grim. I hadn't graduated from high school and was an ex-con. I had no skills and a bad attitude. Then my probation officer told me about some local businessmen who were hiring guys like me—taking a chance. I met Howard Rawlings, and he hired me to work in the warehouse. I let him down a few times in the beginning. I was late, didn't show up for work, screwed up orders, that kind of thing. Howard could have fired me, but he didn't. He counseled me, encouraged me to get my GED, and slowly, I became the man and employee he knew I could be. I rose from loading trucks and pulling stock to shift supervisor. Then, I was promoted to assistant manager, and finally to full warehouse manager."

Walt blinks hard, makes a sound in his throat, and takes a sip of coffee. "I got married, had two kids, and sent them to college. Rook, I was at a crossroads when I was twenty-one. Without your uncle, I'd be in prison, or dead. Howard Rawlings is my hero."

I'm struggling with my own emotions but try to help Walt regain his composure. "What a great story. I'm so glad I ran into you. Are those pictures of your family?" I gesture to framed photos on the desk. Walt nods and points out his wife, son, daughter, and their families. He tells me he's a grandfather of five, loves to fish, but his passion is still his job. He segues enthusiastically into how the product line has grown over the years, how they've introduced new technology to the warehouse, added to the fleet, emphasized training and customer relationships.

I glance at the items on Walt's desk and shelves and sit up straight, staring at a small plastic model of a Buckeye Brands delivery truck, bearing the logo, graphics, and slogan I'd seen a thousand times.

"Walt, does Buckeye Brands do business with Ohio State?" I hold my breath.

"Sure do. They're a big customer. Howard got that relationship going in the '60s. Why?"

"Bishop and I took a tour of the Horseshoe the other day, and I think I saw one of the company's trucks parked under the stadium. What do you sell them?"

"Well, let's see. Cleaning supplies for dorms and offices—a lot of those. Also landscaping products, like weed killer and fertilizer. Do you realize how many acres they maintain in grass, flowers, shrubs, and trees? It's probably bigger than the Botanical Gardens. Also paper products—paper towels, plates, cups, toilet paper, napkins. Paint too, for maintenance, signs, lining streets and paths."

My mind is racing. There's something there. I feel it nibbling at my brain. *Come on, Rook. Think. Connect the dots. Get creative. Color outside the lines.* Then, like a flower opening to the sun, I see the idea spread before me, each petal perfectly formed. Paint. Lines. The Horseshoe. Buckeye Brands.

"That truck I saw at the Horseshoe. What was it delivering?"

"Probably paper products, maybe fertilizer for the field and paint for maintenance of the bathrooms and offices. I could look up the order."

"Possibly paint to line the football field?"

"Yes, we provide that. Why?"

"Walt, you said you were sorry you couldn't attend Howard's funeral. I just thought of a way for you to pay tribute to Howard and participate in his funeral. Want to hear?"

Walt nods, and as I talk, his face goes through a series of emotions. I think I catch confusion and shock, but in the end, he breaks into a wide smile, nodding furiously.

Back in the car, I spell out my newly hatched plan to Bishop, who whoops in delight. "That is brilliant, crazy, and pure Howard. I'm in. Call Walt and set it up. The sooner, the better. Of course, there's one big drawback."

"That being?"

"It's irreversible. If it doesn't work, we're screwed."

to do list

- Steel my nerves
- Spread ashes!
- Get Sammie OSU coat to
-   match collar
- Do victory dance in
-   Bishop's backyard
-
-
-
-
-
-

CHAPTER FORTY-ONE

October

Committed

The next morning, appreciating the irony, I ask my sister-in-law for an apron.

Barb—whose apron of the day proclaims, MANY HAVE EATEN HERE. FEW HAVE DIED—is gracious.

"Do you want a particular theme?"

"You choose. Fair warning, it might come back damaged. Give me one you can live without."

Barb rummages in her pantry and returns holding two aprons. "Take your pick." The first one is decorated with a skull and crossbones and says BADASS GRANDMA. The other features artwork of a whip with the inscription: I DO VERY BAD THINGS, BUT I DO THEM VERY WELL.

"I'll take the badass one. I can see why you haven't been wearing these to church functions." I turn to Bishop, casually dressed in jeans and a wool shirt. "Shall we go make history?"

During the ride to Buckeye Brands, the banter from the kitchen evaporates. I tell Bishop, "My bravado is fading. Distract me."

Bishop stops at a red light and glances at me "OK. Let's see. I've been pondering what you told me about your therapy, and I have some thoughts. Interested?"

"Sure. You're a trained professional. An expert."

"We're all influenced by our parents, by our upbringing. But those influences just intensify traits you already have."

I flash on my father's tools hanging in the garage: each one on a specific hook, its shape outlined in white paint. I see his shoes lined up glossy with polish, his carefully folded newspaper, his notebook with the car mileage and oil changes meticulously recorded. "Genetic, you say?"

"Your perfectionism, which you consider some kind of fatal flaw, is just part of who you are."

"I don't want to be flawed. But here's the thing. I'm wired to pursue perfection, which, it turns out, is not a worthy goal. What do I do with that paradox?"

"Welcome to reality. That makes you… exactly like everybody else. We're all caught in a struggle against our personality, trying to release unhealthy behaviors."

"Mmmm." I consider this bit of wisdom. "What's your unhealthy behavior?

"I'm surprised you have to ask. Pride. Not pretty, especially for a spiritual leader."

"I just think of you as confident. Assured."

"Yeah, but then I cross the line from confident to arrogant, proving that old adage that your weaknesses are just your strengths taken too far. It's the same with you. You think your orthodoxy is a flaw. But many times it's you being brave, standing up for what's right. Remember in the book of Acts, it talks about the gifts of the Spirit? Well, I've been watching you for over sixty years, and you have the gift of wisdom and the gift of discernment. Be grateful for them. Like the superheroes say, 'Use your power for good and not for evil.'"

It's a bird! It's a plane! It's Badass Grandma!

Bishop pulls into Buckeye Brands, parks, and takes Uncle Howard's cremains and a video camera out of the backseat. "Let's do this." We enter the building via the loading dock. Walt is there, holding the door open for us. There are handshakes, welcomes, and suddenly we're in front of a work table, where Walt's placed a can of paint, gloves, a strong light, and several tools.

"Walt? Is one can of paint enough? It seems like it's not." I try to do the math, or chemistry, or physics required by this science experiment, but fail.

Walt taps the top of the paint can. "It's enough. Remember, we've been doing this for a long time. Trust me."

I put on Barb's apron. "I'm like the host of a TV cooking show, except this recipe only has two ingredients," I tell my co-conspirators.

Bishop opens the paint and breaks the seal on the cremains. "Look. These are extra fine, almost like flour. Just like Mr. Sadler mentioned. Howard was one step ahead of us."

I touch the paint can and bite my lip as a chill races through me. Max's face bobs before me, bruised and hurt. I've been so wrapped up in my brilliant scheme that I didn't make the connection. *A paint can.*

I bring myself back to the task at hand. "Uh, Walt? We're going to have to pour out a little paint, aren't we? To make room? Walt slides a small bucket onto the table. I heft the can and pour out what I hope is an appropriate amount, about a quart. "Oops. Sorry, Barb, your apron just took one for the team." The apron now reads, B   ASS GRANDMA.

I return to my task, pouring in the ashes, while Bishop stirs. We peer into the can, considering the concoction. "We can't unring that bell," I say and Bishop, intones, "The paint thickens."

I pound the lid back on with a soft mallet. No one notices when I reserve a small amount of ashes in the funeral home box. Those, I've decided, will spend eternity as part of a different piece of real estate than Ohio Stadium. We form a solemn processional, and the three of us exit the building and pile into one of the company trucks. Walt secures the paint can, filled with a one-of-a-kind color I've decided to call Howard's Blend.

"Here's how I've set this up," Walt says when we arrive at the stadium and he drives under the stands and parks. "I told my friend who works on the field maintenance crew, name's Cowboy, that…" At my inquisitive look, he backtracks. "Real name's Jesse, but they call him Cowboy on account of he's from Texas. Anyway, I told Cowboy that you two are making a video to honor the founder of Buckeye Brands, who died recently. As part of the video, you want to show how Buckeye Brands products are used, this being one of the more impressive uses." He gestures to indicate the football field on the other side of the wall.

"That's a good cover story," I say, which sounds immodest since I invented it.

"I said you'd love to handle the striper, but he said no way. Not for the biggest university in the country, for a game that will be televised to millions of people. Those lines have to be one hundred percent straight and not..." Here he waves his hand like a snake weaving through the grass. "He said you could walk alongside and film but not run the machine. I also told him that the formula for the paint was a tiny bit different in case he noticed a change."

"Good thinking," Bishop says, as he gets out of the truck and grabs the ancient video recorder he unearthed at home to use as a prop. Walt picks up the paint can and leads us single file toward an obscure door marked NO ADMITTANCE.

After all our planning and plotting, I'd counted on a more dramatic final moment. Fireworks. A drumroll. Thunder and lighting. Strobe lights. But like a long labor and a quick delivery, Uncle Howard is committed to the earth or, more accurately, is rolled onto the field in short order.

Playing along with Walt's setup, Bishop pretends to film Cowboy as he pours the paint into the striper and walks slowly and steadily across the field. Cowboy proves to be a colorful character, a retired rodeo bronco rider who migrated north with a girlfriend, found work at the university, and enjoys his role getting the field ready for the participants and spectators, rather than performing himself. "Much better for my health. I broke my arm three times and my shoulder twice," he says, grimacing as he touches these mended parts of himself. "Broncs are mean. Buckeye fans are just..." He laughs and searches for the right word. "Passionate."

Despite his repeatedly broken and reset bones, he lays down remarkably straight lines on the grass. I'm relieved that the paint coming out of the striper is still basically white. *This is working*, I allow myself, *this is actually working.* Then we're done. Cowboy finishes and Bishop makes a tiny fist pump behind Cowboy's back.

Well, it's in the can; I mean, it's out of the bag. I mean, Uncle Howard's out of the can. Whatever. The two men walk off the field, talking about football and rodeos. Lingering, I look at the thousands of empty seats, the flag whipping on its pole in the end zone, the white lines marking off the territory under dispute into ten-yard chunks. I glow with satisfaction at fulfilling Howard's final wish, even though it took some shenanigans. I also feel some apprehension. The diversions of the past few weeks are over.

Football. Chess. Life. Sometimes you play on a team; sometimes you play alone. There are rules, penalties, and consequences. Some, like Knight, come to the game with different abilities, and some, like Michelle, leave the game too early. I've been on the sidelines too long.

Time to rejoin the fray.

to do list

- Give me a D! Give me
- an O!
- Give me an N! Give me E!
- What's it spell?
- DONE!
- Wash Barb's apron
- Pack for CO
-
-
-
-
-

CHAPTER FORTY-TWO

October

Solace

B arb's apron carries a warning: DOES NOT COOK
WELL WITH OTHERS.

Barb has put out an elaborate afternoon tea to
celebrate our success at the field. Bishop begs off, and goes to
Woodbridge to work, leaving Barb and me to drink tea from
dainty cups and partake of tiny sandwiches and bite-sized cakes.
We toast Uncle Howard. I describe Cowboy. Barb tells funny
stories about the dental office where she works and shares an
Abernathy anecdote that has me shaking my head. Where has
this clever Barb been hiding? I feel ashamed of my past opinion
of her. I always thought she was sweet but did not "think great
thoughts," as the Scarecrow in *The Wizard of Oz* put it. It's like
discovering that the everyday picture hanging in the hall you
think is a print is an original masterpiece.

"Oh my, I've got to finish up dinner. Mom's joining us tonight," Barb says. Barb's mother, Irene Burke, lives in a nearby retirement community and comes over for dinner once a week. Nearly ninety, Irene is a tall woman with thinning white hair and a ramrod bearing. I've met her many times over the years. Bishop considers her an excellent mother-in-law.

"Rook, can you do me a favor?" Barb calls from the kitchen while I set the dining room table. "Bishop is picking Mom up, but later on tonight he has a church meeting and I promised a neighbor I'd give her a ride to the hospital, and that's in the opposite direction from Mom's complex. Could *you* drive Mom home around 7 p.m.?"

"Happy to," I say, lining up the silverware. Hearing Bishop and Irene at the back door, I leave the table to say hello. A few minutes later, Bishop, winking, hands me a highball glass full of crushed ice, whiskey, and Coke. "Your prescription is ready, madam."

After dinner, driving Irene home, I ask about life at the retirement village. "What gets you up every day?"

"Breakfast! What I mean is having a routine. I get dressed for meals. I play bingo, and I attend most of the concerts and lectures they put on for us. I usually write some cards and letters every day, go to exercise classes, church, and watch some TV."

We arrive at the circular drive in front of Irene's complex. I start to open my door so that I can walk her inside, but she grabs my hand and stops me. "Barb's told me about your last few months. I went through something similar many years ago. I don't usually share this story, but I want to share it with you. Would that be all right?" I murmur my assent.

"This happened when I was ten. I grew up on a farm in Illinois, and there were eight of us kids. My parents were always busy. They worked hard to keep us fed and clothed and in school."

I close my eyes and picture a hardscrabble farm with a dirt yard, a chicken coop, and kids riding a pony in a meadow. This scene is heavily influenced by my reading all the *Little House on the Prairie* books to Jay when he was a boy, but I suppose it's accurate enough.

"One day just before Thanksgiving, my mother was washing clothes and asked me to watch my youngest brother, Will. He was three that year." Irene stops. I think she might have changed her mind about sharing her past, but she resumes, although the pace of her narrative slows with each sentence.

"I took Will and my doll and we went to one of the pastures to watch the cows. I got absorbed in balancing my doll on a low branch when I realized I hadn't heard Willy for a bit and looked around for him. He wasn't in sight."

Irene grips my hand tighter and squeezes it. "Willy had somehow managed to climb the steps to a stock water tank. I think he wanted to sail a piece of wood he'd found. He leaned too far over it, fell in, and—he drowned. While I was supposed to be watching him."

I gulp air, trying to stop my tears. Irene sighs. "Imagine the guilt I felt. I wanted to die. Then my mother gave me a great gift. She took me in her arms and told me she loved me, she forgave me, and that together we'd get through the grief and whatever came after. She asked me to live every day I was given with love and kindness, to honor Willy."

I'm crying hard now: over this story, over my own story, over the stories of all sad and bereft people. Irene continues, her voice firmer now. "My brother's been dead eighty years, but I think of him every day. I've tried to live as my mother asked, with happiness, joy, and love."

Irene sits quietly while I sob. She gives my hand a final squeeze.

"Rook dear, God's grace is wide. Avail yourself of it."

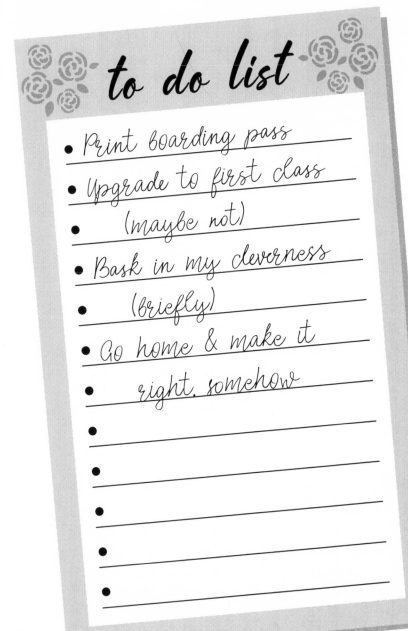

to do list

- Print boarding pass
- Upgrade to first class
- (maybe not)
- Bask in my cleverness
- (briefly)
- Go home & make it
- right, somehow

CHAPTER FORTY-THREE

October

Advice

The silence builds.

Bishop is driving me to the Columbus airport, and with the intuition of a master counselor, leaves me to my own thoughts. As we take the final exit, I tell him, "I liked spending time with you."

"Likewise. What's your frame of mind going back?"

"Confused."

"I have to report that I've caught a whiff of self-pity coming from you."

I'm dumbstruck. "Well, damn, brother. I thought you were…" Tears form and I stop talking. Bishop has cut me off at the knees.

Bishop gives me some verbal space, but he clearly has something he wants to say. Why did he wait until we were practically at the departures zone?

"Look, you have a storybook life. An abundance of gifts. You're smart and clever. You have a great family, financial security, and good health. The way I see it, you've lost your perspective. You're whining about how bad the world is treating you when instead, you should be down on your knees thanking God for your blessings. I couldn't let you go back to Colorado without some tough love. Quit focusing on what isn't perfect. Love, forgive, accept. Do that and all will be well."

I want to react, but oddly, I can't muster up much emotion. Wine experts describe a complex vintage using multiple adjectives: buttery, bright, austere. I'm a complex vintage myself, and right now I'm layered, dense, contradictory, and just plain tired.

Bishop isn't done. "You made a mistake, sis. That's OK. Forgive yourself. I do. So does Campbell. So does Jay, really. God certainly does."

I'm quiet, going over his words. "I want to believe what you're saying. My ears hear you say there's forgiveness, but all I feel in here…" I tap my chest. "All I feel is condemnation."

"That's your own tape playing. Change it. Seriously, I'm begging you. You made a mistake. Don't compound things by making an even bigger one. Pushing away the people who love you is not the answer."

"I want to change it. I do. It's just… it was such a… you've never—"

He cuts me off. "That's exactly what I'm talking about. 'I'm the worst.' 'I'm unforgivable.' That's bullshit, and your pathetic act is wearing thin. I expect better of you." Bishop's voice has acquired edges and ridges that cause me to cross my arms over my chest.

I'm shocked at Bishop's words. If this is a message of love and forgiveness, he forgot some key ingredients. *Like love and forgiveness.* My brain forms a retort, but I clamp my teeth together.

"Rook. I'm in the advice business, and with you, I can deliver that advice straight up. I imagine you don't want to hear what I'm saying, but maybe on down the road, it'll resonate." Bishop pulls up in front of the United sign. I drown out the rest of his speech by hopping out and slamming the door. I've wrestled my suitcase out of the backseat before he can even come around to my side of the car.

"Thanks for the ride. I'm glad we were able to get the ashes thing done. Not sure when I'll be back." I deliver this in a rush, desperate to get away from my brother and his *advice.* I give him a soft punch on the arm, turn, and holding one hand out in a stiff goodbye salute, head into the terminal. I don't look back.

An hour later, I'm seated at the departure gate with a copy of *USA Today*, a Starbucks, and a protein bar. The plane is on time, and in a few hours, I get to re-enter the Colorado version of Rook's Life. According to a recent critic, I'm doing a less-than-stellar job in the title role. *Well, screw him. Who made him an authority?*

My phone rings. Campbell. *Great. Another critic.* "Hello. I'm at the airport."

"Ah, yeah. I thought... call... and... plane. So... time... process, and..." My husband's voice fades.

"Campbell, I can't hear you very well. What? What do you want? We're boarding now."

"Sammie... ost... can't..." The line goes dead.

I put away my phone and head for the gate. Something about Sammie. He probably can't find something. Her leash? Her heartworm pill? Can't understand her body language? Expecting a grown man to take care of a small dog is apparently too much to ask.

Whatever it is, it'll have to wait. I'm on my way home. I'll fix things for Campbell, and for Sammie.

Who's going to fix things for me?

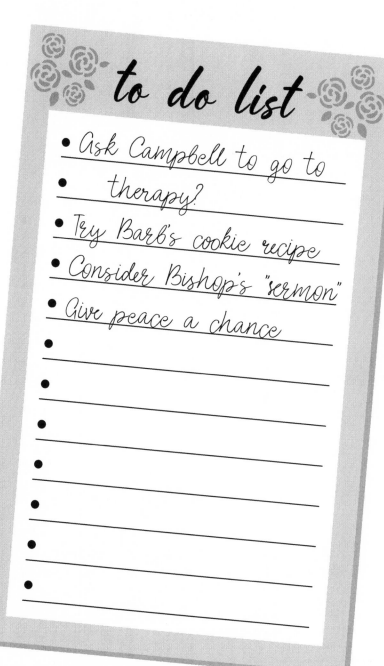

to do list

- Ask Campbell to go to therapy?
- Try Barb's cookie recipe
- Consider Bishop's "sermon"
- Give peace a chance

CHAPTER FORTY-FOUR

October

Wounded

I t's too quiet.

On the drive home from the airport, I wrestle with how to approach Campbell. Normally, we'd celebrate my success in Ohio with a special Debrief and snack, or maybe go out to dinner, but these aren't normal times.

Campbell meets me in the garage and grabs my suitcase from the backseat. He's subdued, and I follow him into the house, puzzled. We're definitely off-script. He drops my bag near the stairs and sits down heavily at the kitchen table. *Something's not right.* I slide in opposite him. Now the silence in the house rivets my attention. "Where's Sammie?"

Campbell lifts his head to face me. "I lost her."

"You – what?"

"She's missing. That's what I was trying to tell you on the phone."

Something cold clutches at my heart, and I swallow and stare at my husband. "I don't ..."

But I do. I understand it all in an instant. I entrusted sweet Sammie to this incompetent bumbler, and the worst has come about. "What happened?" This comes out as a whisper.

"I was stupid. I was going to the mailbox, so I tried to put her leash on, but she kept dancing away from me and it was becoming a big hairy deal, so I let her go commando. She walked along with me just fine, then I ran into a neighbor at the mailboxes who wanted to talk about the dues and the upcoming homeowners association election, and I... ." Campbell talks fast, as if he thinks his torrent of words will wash away his neglect. "I forgot about her."

"You forgot about her." My face is hardening into a mask, but inside my thoughts are racing. Every scene I envision is horrific. Sammie run over by a car. Sammie caught in the jaws of a coyote. Sammie falling down some hole in the ground.

"Just for a minute. A couple of minutes. Then I called and called, but she had vanished. I yelled *treat* which usually gets a response, but nothing. It was getting dark, so I got a flashlight and spent the next hour combing the meadow and our yard, but either she was hiding, or - I don't know. How could she disappear so quickly?"

He stumbles on. "I looked hard everywhere last night and today, but let's do it again, together. Honey, I'm so sorry." There's anguish in his voice. "She'll come to you. I bet she's crouched under a rock waiting to hear your voice. We'll look till we find her. I'm so, so sorry."

I bow my head. Normally, I'd explode at such a colossal screw-up. Instead, my silence is absorbed into the larger, eerie silence of the house. I feel my heart grow smaller, like a reverse Grinch. Smaller, smaller, smaller, until it's a black hole, a pinpoint of dark matter, pulling in all the love and good feelings within its gravitational field and crushing them.

I get up. My sixty-two years, which I wear lightly, bear me down. I feel old. Tired. Defeated. I go to the pantry and stuff some of Sammie's treats in my pockets. I have no expectation of ever seeing her again, but I'll take the right steps. Campbell trails me out the door, unsure of where he stands, desperate for a sign. I ignore him.

Two hours later, I return to the house and start making posters. I remember Bishop's story about Ranger, but I know this saga will not have a happy ending. I call our vet, neighbors, area animal shelters, and the local weekly newspaper to place a notice in the Classifieds. I call the national registry where I enrolled Sammie and her microchip number when she was a puppy.

I sit in the family room, where my hand goes to the space in the chair beside me, and my fingers work the fabric. *Sammie's spot*. To the awful visuals that I keep picturing, I add a soundtrack: Sammie whimpering and crying.

I hear Campbell in the kitchen, fumbling with pans, as he attempts to scratch together some dinner for us. The parallels of our respective situations are not lost on me. I get it. I was careless and my innocent grandson suffered as a result. I want forgiveness and a way forward. Campbell … yada, yada, yada.

Appreciation for Jay's recent behavior floods through me. It feels good to hurl thunderbolts when something inexplicable has happened. The world has handed me lemons, so I'm going to make, not lemonade, but lemon pies to throw at everyone. *Smack.*

The evening passes slowly. Campbell tries to initiate several conversations, but I'm not up to *processing* what happened and how I'm feeling. I'm not angry. I don't cry. It's more like a void has opened up inside me, and I'm aware of a strange new emotion.

I don't care.

to do list

- Search
- Call shelters again
- Put up posters
- Make appt. w/ Dr. Canon
- Find it in my heart to
-     forgive Campbell, but
-     first
- Find my heart
-
-
-
-

CHAPTER FORTY-FIVE

October

Revelation

I'm too agitated to lie down on Dr. Canon's stupid couch.

I defy him by sitting in a chair and looking him full in the face. I'm going to expose the Wizard. Prove he's a fake, with absolutely no solutions. He just wants to hand out challenges and quests as he hides behind a curtain. He's a fraud.

"You're looking stormy today. What's up?"

"What's up is my careless husband lost my dog. While I was off in Ohio fulfilling my uncle's last wish, Campbell allowed Sammie to be taken by some wild animal or get herself lost. My dog is dead because of him. He's a…" I jump up and pace to the window.

"Rook, I'm so sorry. You must feel awful." *Right on cue. Empathy.* He's like a jukebox. Punch in the right combination and he spews out some relevant emotion. I want to punch *him*, all right. Directly in his smug little Freudian face.

"Awful? That's an understatement. I can't sleep thinking about her. How she suffered. How she cried. It's just one more…"

"One more, what?"

"One more hurt. One more example of how the world lets me down. One more innocent victim, betrayed by the people who are supposed to keep us safe."

"Keep *us* safe?"

"Uh, I meant keep her… I mean…" I twirl from the window. "Quit confusing me!"

"So someone was supposed to keep you safe, and they failed?"

"What are you asking? I'm talking about—oh my God! You are so infuriating."

"No, I want you to follow this emotion. Whose job is it to keep us safe?"

"Our parents, of course. And mine did. I wasn't kidnapped or stolen awa…" I stop. Stare at him. Images crowd in. Big double doors. A long, echoing hallway. A sickening, sour smell. A small black-and-white TV bolted to the wall high up near the ceiling.

"I…"

"Tell me what you are seeing right now," Dr. Canon instructs me.

"It's the place where we visited my brother when I was a kid."

"You mean Bishop? A camp? His college dorm?"

"No. My other brother. Knight."

"You haven't said much about him. Where did you visit him?"

"The state school. In Columbus. Where my parents put him when he was six."

"Put him?"

"They placed him in the state school when he was six. I was almost five. They thought it would have the resources, staff, and, you know, knowledge to help him reach his potential."

When Knight was growing up in the 1940s, there were no programs for children with Down syndrome. Parents either kept their children at home or put them in state-run institutions. It was only later that other options emerged.

"What was that like for you?"

"Horrible. Noisy. Smelly. I hated it. We went there to pick him up for holidays, vacations, and special celebrations, like birthdays. But taking him back was the worst."

"Why?"

I sink into my memories. I imagine being a little girl with two older brothers, who eat dinner with me, play with me, take walks with me, and love me. Then one of those brothers disappears—there one day and gone the next. Poof. The next time I see that brother he's in a terrible place. No toys, no clothes of his own, sharing a dorm room with dozens of other boys. No mother or father to love him. I collapse onto one of Dr. Canon's chairs, overwhelmed by feelings of loss and confusion.

I'm flat out sobbing now. I wrap my arms around myself. Waves of emotions come at me, crest, and release me to the next onslaught. I shut my eyes and speak to Dr. Canon in gasps.

"I—I'm five years old and my brother…" I heave myself upright and swallow. "My parents put Knight in the state school and oh, it's a bad place. I hate going there. I can see he hates it too. But I can't help him. Why did they send him there?"

"Stay with that, Rook. You're five and your brother has disappeared. No one is helping you understand. Suddenly you see him again, living in a place you think is horrible. What's that like? Just notice what's happening."

I remember how frustrated my parents would get because Knight never had his own clothes when we picked him up. He'd have on too large pants with the name tag BAILEY sewn into the waistband. A shirt with stains that belonged to ANDERSON. My mother would return Knight with new clothes, all carefully marked BROWNLEE, but the next time we came, those clothes would be MIA, and Knight would look like a refugee.

I watch my brother on the steps of the state school growing smaller and smaller as we drive away. My mother is crying, after prying Knight's fingers off the car door and leaving him with one of the matrons. My father is clenching the steering wheel in a fierce grip, while Bishop, next to me, is staring out the window, his face a mask. "I think... I think he must have done something bad, and I'm scared if I do something bad, my parents will put me there too. I'd better be extra good so I can stay with my Mom and Dad."

"Are you afraid? Confused?"

"I don't understand. Is he being punished? He must have broken one of dad's rules. I don't want to go to that nasty place, so... so I'd better be perfect. I'd better follow all the rules. Be a good girl and obey my teachers and parents." Even as I speak, I can hear the little kid fear in my voice. *Be good, be good.*

I'm sitting up straight now. My chest hurts, but the waves of feelings are slowing. I have a sense of connecting the dots of a puzzle. I take a deep breath, let it out, and look at Dr. Canon, who says, "A big sigh. What was that?"

"Crying. It's just exhausting. Was that—uh—was that an epiphany?"

"It's certainly an important connection, finding—"

I interrupt. "My poor brother. How could my parents do that? How could my *mother* do that? She was the most loving, caring—how could she leave her son in a place like that?"

"You seem to be focusing on her role. Why?"

"Because in nature, mothers are the ones who stay with their young. They guard them, protect them, and fight for them. I loved my Mom. I know she loved all of us, all three of us. I don't understand how she could..."

Dr. Canon is looking intently at me. "If your mother and father were here right now, what would you tell them?"

I picture my parents in a therapist's office. No, not their style. Rev. Leatherman's office, maybe. I see my mother's sweet face, my father's stern one. I never confronted my parents over much of anything. Mom and I disagreed about the length of my skirts in high school, but not much else, and you did not talk back to Frank Brownlee. Period.

"I guess I'd tell them they should have kept Knight at home." I squint at my parents' faces to see how they're taking this criticism. "I'd tell them I didn't like going there. I'd tell them Knight was probably terrified and cried his eyes out every day. I bet when they brought him home for a visit he thought it was permanent and when they took him back, it broke his heart all over again." My mother is crying into a handkerchief; my father's eyebrows are knotting together in what all the Brownlee children recognized as the precursor to a storm.

"Rook, it's completely understandable you'd want to say that. It's OK. You can own those feelings. You can share those feelings. Now, what would they say back to you?"

I stop. I imagine being the mother of a child with Down syndrome in the 1940s. They'd brought their new son home and six weeks later found out he would never develop like their firstborn, Bishop. A shocking surprise. The doctor had been brutal, "Have another child. This one is hopelessly retarded." Elizabeth Brownlee had mothered Knight as lovingly and tenderly as she had her oldest and later her youngest child. But she had no one to understand or help or console her. That's when she'd stumbled onto her life verse, paging through her Bible. Romans 8:28. Her lifeline. *God works all things together for the good of those who love him.*

My answer to Dr. Canon is halting. "I guess they'd tell me I couldn't possibly appreciate what it was like. The toll it took on my mother. On their marriage. That Knight was a perpetual toddler—running away, hiding in the doghouse, knocking over lamps. Once, he got in my dad's car and put it in gear. It rolled into our yard and narrowly missed me, playing in the sandbox. Another time, he broke away from Bishop and me, ran into the street, and almost got hit. In other words, he required constant supervision. They'd say they were counseled to put Knight in that school. They were told he'd do well there, that he'd learn what he could, be with other children, be taught the skills he needed. That it seemed like the best possible solution."

"Do you believe that?"

"I believe it seemed true to them at the time. But now, looking back, all I can see is Knight being sacrificed for the family."

"And how does that make you feel?"

"Guilty. Guilty as hell." I gulp air, manage not to cry. "Also, ashamed. Like my parents had done something awful. I was careful never to share what they'd done with anybody. Our family's secret shame. Not that they had a child with a disability, but that they put that child out of sight."

Dr. Canon gives me a sympathetic look. "So you protected your parents instead of the other way around."

"But see, just you saying that makes me more ashamed, like my parents weren't good parents. They were good parents! They just had a, kind of a *Sophie's Choice* situation."

I lean back, exhausted. The session is ending, and for once I'm not ready to run out the door. Dr. Canon is telling me to be gentle with myself, but I'm already remapping my life, revisiting important decisions, and reevaluating my relationships based on this new insight. I feel a strong urge to share this discovery with Campbell, then remember we're barely speaking. The confidante of choice is obvious. Bishop.

An eye witness.

to do list

- Research about Columbus state school
- Keep up CP
- Forgive us our debts as we forgive our debtors
- Oh Sammie
-
-
-
-
-
-

CHAPTER FORTY-SIX

October

Comfort

I watch the tips of my hiking boots appear and disappear, appear and disappear.

I'm hiking a two-mile trail at Elk Meadow Park on this early October morning. I have the trail largely to myself. I'm only occasionally passed by a runner; most of them are accompanied by large, panting dogs. I'm glad of the solitude. I'm headed to a bench at a fork in the trail to spend a quiet hour taking stock.

It's only going to reach forty-five degrees today, and the chill of a mountain morning in late fall makes my breath visible until it mingles with the lingering fog. I am glad I've worn my parka, wool hat, and mittens.

My thoughts swirl like the leaves in a small open spot to my right, dancing in the slight breeze. Michelle's been dead a month. Sammie gone a week. Three days since my Knight revelation. I realize getting older means saying goodbye to so many people who are part of my story. People I've loved, people I've lost. My parents, Knight, Uncle Howard, a long list of relatives, Michelle. Those with me still: Bishop, Barb, Campbell, Jay, Carly, Max. All part of my story.

When Jay was a little boy, getting ready for bed, he'd beg, "Mom, read me a story. Tell me a story." Everybody loves a good story. My cloud of witnesses would want my life to be a good story: action-packed, funny, tender, and with a triumphant ending. They wouldn't mind if their heroine had a few setbacks, but they didn't want me going in the ditch permanently.

Looking through a gap in the pines, I see a cluster of slow-moving dots down in the meadow about a mile away. Elk. The trail rises steadily, but I'm in good shape and I reach my destination in forty minutes. I sit, studying the landscape. Here the trail splits. One path bends and continues upward, and the other slopes down to the meadow. This bench occupies the middle ground. Good for contemplation.

I picture myself getting to the top of Bergen Peak, another hour up the trail. I hoist myself up those last few feet, reach the summit, and encounter God, sitting cross-legged in the middle of a clearing. He's wearing an apron that proclaims him TOP CHEF. Of course.

Well God, here I am on the mountaintop. I've come to meet you and get some help.

I'm surprised when God answers. "You didn't have to hike up here to find me. I was right there in your kitchen. But this is nice too."

I'm trying to sort out some things. Michelle's death. Knight in the state school. Uncle Howard's money. Any advice?

There's a long silence, and I catch myself thinking, *See, these are hard issues.* Then I remember that God knows exactly what I'm thinking and quickly revise my thought to, *Take all the time you need.*

The silence continues. God's doing the same thing as Dr. Canon: keeping quiet so that I'll talk. I decide to wait him out. I notice a movement to my left and turn to see a squirrel digging in the dirt. *That's one,* I count, playing the trifecta game automatically. A new thought occurs. I also play the *perfecta* game every day: trying not to make a false move, obeying all the rules. Bishop thinks I have a natural tendency towards perfectionism. *Maybe.* At least now, after my revelation in therapy, I know why that tendency got solidified into a hard-core outlook on life.

Does that help? *It does.* Self-knowledge is a good thing. I might not make radical changes in my behavior at this point in my life, but I'm beginning to believe that I can understand those behaviors, apologize for them, and make tiny corrections. I picture Sammie on her leash, pulling so hard against her collar that she choked and gagged. I do the same thing— pulling hard in the direction I want to go, a direction that's not the best path. The thought of Sammie creates an almost physical pain in my chest, and I shove it away.

Tight and loose. Campbell often talks about tight and loose in his job. He tells his staff, "Now this is tight: You must review lunchroom expectations with your class. But what's loose is that you can do it at a place and time and manner that work for you."

Campbell says another thing I like. He stumbled onto his little catchphrase three years ago, and it so delights me that he trots it out frequently. After a minor tussle or sharp exchange about some failing of his, he says, "I'm sorry. I was wrong. I'll never do it again." *Hilarious!* Why had it taken him so many years to find the precise words I was longing to hear?

My impatience gets the better of me, and I cave. *Father, apparently I need to tighten something and loosen something. I'm pretty sure I know which is which. But knowing it and doing it are two different things, so that's what I need help with.*

God is still sitting comfortably in the clearing, smiling at me. A congregation of one. I remember squirming in the pews of the Presbyterian church as a child, restless and twitchy during the long service. My mother would take my hand and gently trace the tip of her index finger along my small fingers: up over the ends, down into the spaces between, over and over until I was practically in a trance.

I smile back at God, at the tender memory of my mother, as my shoulders soften and my breathing grows regular. I think of my 'mother's heartache over Knight, Campbell's alcoholism, and circle back to Michelle Hammond. Everyone carries sadness, grief, pain. Some hide it, others share it, but everyone feels it. God must get tired of watching his people stumble around, confused and bereft, getting everything wrong, making terrible choices, and then whining that he's nowhere to be found—when he's right there, in the clearing, waiting.

An old hymn drifts into my mind. We sang it at my father's memorial service, and it always puts a lump in my throat.

Be still, my soul! The Lord is on thy side;
Bear patiently the cross of grief or pain;
Leave to thy God to order and provide;
In every change He faithful will remain.
Be still, my soul! Thy best, thy heavenly Friend
Through thorny ways leads to a joyful end.

Then I know. Hold tight to God and loosely to your pain. Hold tight to others and loosely to your judgments. I turn to see that God has joined me on the bench. "Father, I'm sorry. I was wrong. But I'm pretty sure I'll do it again." God doesn't speak.

He just takes my hand and caresses my fingers.

to do list

- <u>Breathe</u>
- <u>Call Bishop about state</u>
- <u>school</u>
- <u>Stitch</u>
- <u>Take a tiny step</u>

CHAPTER FORTY-SEVEN

October

Homework

Ziggy delays his entrance for dramatic effect.

I sit on the couch and study Dr. Canon's artwork: a soothing seascape, an abstract in blues and greens, and a photograph of two mountain peaks near Aspen called the Maroon Bells.

Dr. Canon comes in, sits in his usual chair, and gets down to business. Sensing his moment, Ziggy shoots from behind the drapes and leaps onto the back of the couch, where he spreads himself out behind my neck like a fur boa. I can feel his tail tapping my shoulder in a lazy rhythm, and when I turn my head, he's regarding me with half slit eyes, whiskers twitching.

"Does Ziggy ever sit in your lap, Dr. Canon?"

"Once in a while, but Ziggy has great instincts. He earns his tuna. Have you been thinking about our last session?"

"All the time. I come at it from different angles, try to see if it still makes sense, and it does, but in a way, so what? Every child has stuff happen to them, or to the people around them. Accidents, death, abuse, illness, violence. I'm not special in having been hurt or for suffering a traumatic event in my childhood. Anyway, what can I do about it? My parents are dead. Knight is dead. I can't undo what happened when I was a kid."

"Understanding the child you used to be can help you understand the adult you are now. Let's consider how that understanding can make a difference in your life."

"And while I'm at it," I quip, "do you want me to solve the problem of world peace?"

"I notice you use your humor as a way to move away from tender feelings." His tone is warm, the observation neutral, yet I feel a flush of embarrassment.

"Do I? See, even that comment makes me feel like I did something wrong. That I'm not being serious enough, not being a good patient. That I'm disappointing you." I entwine my fingers together. Force my hands into my lap.

Dr. Canon is silent, but the silence is comfortable. I let some time go by, unclench my hands, and try to remember what I'm supposed to be doing. Oh yes, understand my little-girl self.

"Well, let's see. Poor little Rook. She has a traumatic experience as a child and decides to do everything by the book. Not that that's a bad thing," I say, but Dr. Canon holds me in a steady gaze. I bite back my next jest: *little Rook, by the book*. "OK, so of course, she takes it too far and grows up to become a one-woman enforcement squad. It's not enough that she follows the rules. She has to make sure everybody else does too. How am I doing so far?"

Dr. Canon says nothing. *So infuriating.* I bow to his authority and take up the thread of my analysis. "She tries to never make mistakes and develops both a ready set of scathing judgments and the poor social skills to use them on her victims. In other words, she becomes a Class A Bitch."

"Rook, stop. That's exactly the kind of self-loathing we're trying to eradicate. I want you to rephrase that with more empathy for yourself."

This session should have been a victory lap to celebrate my newly discovered self-knowledge. Instead, Dr. Canon is spoiling my good time and not appreciating my jokes or sarcasm. In a clipped tone I say, "To rephrase, Rook—I mean, I—suffered an event in my childhood that made me stuff down my feelings. I compensated by trying to always be in control and do the right thing, because if I don't—well something bad is going to happen."

"You're angry. Can you tell me why?"

"I feel angry because this is a hopeless cycle. I'm a bitch, and when I realize that about myself, it's just one more way I'm not achieving the perfection I want, so there I go, around again."

"Let's figure out a way to break that cycle and slow this down. There's a lot more going on underneath that equation you just spelled out."

"How does a person develop a whole new personality at age sixty-two"

"It isn't a whole new personality but a part of you that you had to shut down. It's rediscovering parts of yourself and practicing new behaviors and thoughts. For example, being curious about what's under that urge to judge."

I close my eyes. *This is so hard!* My teeth ache from being tightly clenched. I consciously relax them. Bring my shoulders down to a normal level instead of bunched up around my ears. Take a breath. Concentrate on the assignment.

"I don't just feel an urge to judge. It's more like..." I struggle to find the right words. "It's like I'm trying to make things fair, to bring about justice. Sounds like the slogan for a superhero: Truth and Justice."

"It is," said Dr. Canon. "It was Superman's slogan: the never-ending battle for truth, justice, and the American way."

"So I'm not a Class A Bitch? I'm Super Bitch?"

Dr. Canon laughs out loud. I congratulate myself.

"You observe someone being unfair or unjust or breaking the rules. You want to intervene, speak up, right the wrong. Can you picture a different way to react, based on what you now know about yourself?"

"I guess I could stop and ask myself, 'What am I really feeling?' Is the issue that important? Could I let it go? Could I figure out a way to feel compassion for the perp—" Here I look at my therapist and risk another joke. "Probably changing my language from perpetrator to person might help a little." I'm rewarded with a smile. Encouraged, I plunge on. "I guess one way to interrupt the cycle is to allow myself to fail and realize it isn't the end of the world. Should I start breaking some rules?"

Dr. Canon seemed energized by my ramblings. "Give me some rules you could break."

"Well, baby steps, right? Let's see. I don't want to litter. I don't want to get a parking ticket. I'm not comfortable cutting in line at the bank or post office. They'd have to be little rules— like I could wear stripes and plaids together?" Seeing my therapist's face, I amend my comments. "OK, I'll cut out the humor. Sorry. Lifelong habit. I can't think of any rules I want to break right now, but I'll be on the lookout for one. Honest."

"Rook," Dr. Canon says, "we're not looking to kill off your personality, which I happen to think is a very appealing and highly functioning one. Let's just make a few tweaks so that you aren't so hard on yourself, and others."

"Mmmm." I hum, my usual self-soothing behavior.

"Can you take that in? What I just said?"

I'm searching for a funny comeback and stop. Let myself hear the words "appealing and highly functioning." Someone who knows my imperfections is expressing his approval. A voice speaks in my head, *Yeah, but you paid...*

"Yes. I'm trying to accept that compliment."

"What are you feeling about your parents?"

"Conflicted. Especially about my mother. Adult Rook can see why they did what they did. Little-Kid Rook? That's harder. She's a stubborn little girl who holds grudges."

"Adult Rook may have to give Little-Kid Rook some help."

I hum some more. My list of assignments from Dr. Canon is growing:

- Quit using humor to hide my feelings.
- Break some rules.
- Help my inner child forgive my ~~parents~~ mother.

This could take the rest of my life.

"We have a few more minutes, and I want to explore another topic. Has your insight about your brother brought you to better understand your reaction to the accident and to Michelle Hammond?"

I stop humming. "I've thought about that a lot. Before we go there, I want to tell you more about Knight. The state school closed when he was eighteen, and following that, he lived in a series of group homes. The last one, the Franklin County Group Home, was great. He lived there for over twenty years. The people in charge were loving; he shared a room with a roommate, had friends, and worked at a nearby sheltered workshop. They were a family, with dinners together, movies, popcorn, CDs, chores, and he had lots of visits from Mom and Dad, Bishop, and me. I think he knew he was loved." My voice drops lower. "So his story had a better ending than the beginning."

"And what's it like for you to know that?"

It's quiet in the room, and Ziggy stretches out a furry paw to tap my shoulder. His observations on the session are so obvious they might as well be displayed above his head in a thought balloon: "A breakthrough. Hurrah! About time. My, what a good therapy cat I am."

"I feel happy, imagining him as part of that family group."

"It sounds like Knight was a strong person, who suffered through some tough times, but didn't become a victim. He took his fair share of contentment from life. He'd want you to do the same."

I stare at my therapist. "Huh. Knight overcoming the obstacles. A life of victory, not sadness. I've been stuck in this one groove, playing the same song over and over." I meditate on this while Ziggy purrs and Dr. Canon makes notes.

"Rook, tell me what's happening right now for you as you touch your heart." I look up to see Dr. Canon holding his hand over his heart and, looking down, see he's imitating my gesture.

"I feel this sense of contentment. Of peace. That Knight was OK. He knew he was loved. I've been carrying around some unresolved sadness about Knight, the feeling that he paid the price while I got a pass. And I feel the same about the accident. Two seconds' difference and I could be the one with the brain injury, or, heaven forbid, Max. It's just so arbitrary. Maybe all the tears I've been crying for Michelle are really the tears I never shed for Knight."

"I believe your grief will lessen and become manageable, especially now that you've let yourself feel the link between these two events. Rook, I want to give you an assignment. The next time you're faced with a situation where your tape is shouting, 'Be a good girl! Don't break the rules or something bad will happen,' I want you to take a deep breath and make another choice. See what happens. Make a mistake."

Be a bad girl. I picture Sandy in *Grease* swapping out her conservative sweater and skirt for black leather pants and high heels. Dangerous and sexy and thrilling.

"OK, I'll try. But what do I do about Campbell? We love each other, but right now, we don't like each other very much. Plus, we know just how to push each other's buttons."

"What do you want to do about it?"

"Well, fix it. I mean, are you suggesting let it go?"

"I'm suggesting you are two adults who have choices. What choice interests you?"

"We still disagree about the money. We're in a deadlock."

He's silent and lets my words hang in the air until they start to sound foolish and untrue. "Well, we haven't talked about it for a while. I guess I could bring it up and see if he's changed. OK, strike that. See if we could work out a solution. But first, we'd have to enjoy being in the same room."

Dr. Canon gathers his materials to indicate time's up. "I'm confident you can bring that about, and I look forward to hearing about it at our next session. Don't forget that marriage counseling is an option."

"Thanks, but we know what to do; we just don't want to do it."

"When the stakes get high enough, I suspect you'll find your motivation."

That last comment stays with me as I drive home. *Sounds like AA.* Got to hit rock bottom before you want to change. *But Campbell's so infuriating. Not listening. Being so sure of himself. Not at all bothered by making mistakes.*

I suck in my breath. *Am I jealous because he can so easily move past his errors?*

While I obsess over mine.

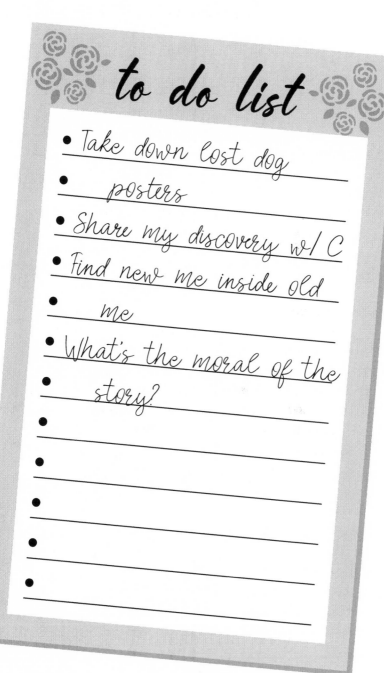

to do list

- Take down lost dog
-    posters
- Share my discovery w/ C
- Find new me inside old
-    me
- What's the moral of the
-    story?

CHAPTER FORTY-EIGHT

October

Stuck

s this the new dynamic?

I'm folding laundry when Campbell yells from the office, "Help! My spreadsheet has gone wonky."

I march into the office, lean over him, and hit a couple of keys. "There. Fixed. Just like the other times I've shown you how."

"You don't have to make me feel like an idiot."

"You're not an idiot. So why put on the helpless routine?"

His voice gets louder. "Why's it a big deal to help me? You're better at this computer stuff than I am. Sorry to be such a pain in the ass."

"What's a pain is when you ask the same thing over and over. It must be nice to have someone around who remembers everything, knows where everything is, and knows how everything works. I'm sick of being that person."

He stands up. Glares. "You're sick of being that person? Well, I'm sick of being this guy. Understanding your moods. Waiting for your therapy to show some results. But no, it's still the same sad, depressed Rook. Like you're the only person who ever had shit happen to them. And it didn't even happen to you. It happened to Max and Michelle Hammond."

I don't know how I can be furious and cry at the same time, but I do.

"Tears again?" He gets up and starts to brush by me.

"Something did happen at therapy," I whisper.

He stops. Turns. He goes back to the desk and waits for me to get control. I sink into a side chair. I tell him about the Knight revelation. It doesn't sound as dramatic in the retelling. In fact, it sounds lame.

When I finish he says, "That so explains you, following the rules, policing the world. I can't believe we never thought of it before. The focus was always on Knight, or your mom and dad, and people paid less attention to you."

"Well, I'd like to think I'm more complicated than that one thing. There are many facets to my warped personality."

He studies me, and my stomach lurches. *What's he thinking?*

"Do you think we can get back to how we were before the accident?" he asks me. "I've been pretty discouraged about how crappy things are around here. And of course, the Sammie thing…"

"I don't want it to be like before," I say, and he sits back, offended. "The way we interacted doesn't work for me anymore. The thing with Knight isn't some magic formula for 'fixing' me. You're not allowed to use it as a template—laying it on top of everything I say or do. The Rook roadmap."

"I didn't think that. Geez, why are you getting upset? See, this is exactly what I mean. We're going along having a perfectly fine conversation, and suddenly, you're pissed. I never know what I did or why you've decided to punish me."

I sigh. "You think every emotion I have is anger. That I'm pissed off, or furious, or seething. There are other emotions, Campbell. There's frustration, disappointment, impatience, confusion, *et cetera*. If you'd listen to me, really listen, you'd figure that out."

He makes an unpleasant noise, which matches the unpleasant look on his face. "You win, Rook. You're the innocent, misunderstood party, and I'm clearly the bad guy. The guy who doesn't listen, who asks too many questions, who interrupts and bothers you. This Knight thing sounded like a way forward, but I see now we're still in deep shit."

I bow my head and bite my lip. *How, oh how, do things go wrong so quickly?*

"Look, I—" The doorbell interrupts my response. I wait for Sammie to hurl herself at the front door, screeching, but the house remains quiet. *Deathly quiet.*

I go to the door, see the UPS man returning to his truck and a small package on the porch. I turn back to Campbell. "I miss Sammie so much."

"I know you do, and you may not believe this, but I do too. I teased you about her, but I enjoyed having her around, except for the barking. The cute way she slept under her blanket, with just her nose poking out. Her Kong obsession. She was a sweet, nice dog, and I'm devastated that I lost her. I know you'll never forgive me. So what do you want to do about us?" He doesn't wait for my answer. Turns away. "Let me know when you figure it out. I'm going to the Club to swim, then grab a burger, and maybe hit a meeting. I assume my being gone will suit you."

Tears sting my eyes but I blink them back. "Fine. Go. Thanks for the discussion." Sarcasm makes the words ugly. "Actually, I'm thinking of going back to Columbus. I want to talk to Bishop about this Knight thing. And I want to talk to my parents."

"Talk to your…" Campbell shrugs, and moments later, I hear his car backing out. My first opportunity to use my newly discovered self-knowledge and I've blown it. *You wanted failure, Dr. Canon? Well, here it is.*

I retrieve the package from the porch. It's addressed to me and contains a pair of silver earrings I admired at the mall weeks ago. The enclosed card reads

To my beautiful wife,

I've missed you and can't wait for you to come home, in every sense.

I love you.
Campbell

to do list

- Visit site of state school
- Wear new earrings
- Wonder as I wander
-
-
-
-
-
-
-
-
-

CHAPTER FORTY-NINE

October

Reconstruction

The building that haunted my childhood is gone.

Bishop and I are parked in front of the site of the demolished Ohio State Institute. In its place is a bland three story building. I ask him, "So, what are these? Offices of some kind?"

"They're still state-owned. I think they're part of the Transportation Department."

"The school that was here, that they tore down—it was so spooky. The boys would reach out to me. Mom said they wanted to touch my blonde hair. The whole thing was horrible."

"Being older, I didn't have the same reaction. I did a little research and the building Knight was in was built right after the Civil War, and it had a Gothic vibe—enormous and forbidding. I can see how it would scare the snot out of a little girl."

"Isn't it amazing—the change from when Knight was little to now? Campbell has children with Down syndrome in his regular classes. There are so many options: group homes, sheltered workshops, special classes at the public schools, therapy, support groups. Mom and Dad had two choices, either keep him home or send him to the state school. Do you think they made the right choice?"

Bishop is quiet for a long time. "The short answer? No. But that's me talking more than fifty years later. If I'd been in their shoes, I can't say what I would have done. I just remember a lot of tears. It wasn't an easy decision."

"Were you embarrassed by Knight? Teased by your friends?"

"Honestly? I was embarrassed, but I was embarrassed by you, too. I was mortified by any younger kid I had to drag along. Typical sibling love-hate relationship." This is Bishop at his best: comforting and genuine.

My relationship with Knight was more complicated. His speech was almost unintelligible, and he spent much of his time talking to himself. Whether that was because of, or despite, living at the state school, I don't know. He was placid, stubborn, and hard to get moving. He could spend an hour folding his pajamas. On visits home, he would take stuff from my room: my favorite eraser, my Girl Scout pin, and most infuriating, the stuffed horse I kept on my pillow. I'd find them in the back of his closet or hidden in his duffel bag. I was the baby sister. Why did I have to be responsible for someone older?

"Bishop, what do you think of my breakthrough in therapy?"

"I guess it just shows how two people can have a completely different take on the same experience. Of course, you were five and I was ten, much better able to process what was happening. See, I don't remember the state school as horrible. Knight had friends there, and I liked their playground a lot. He had toys, he had classes, he got to come home all the time for weekends and vacation."

"So my point-of-view is skewed?"

"More like limited. Just allow that the state school was many things: some good and some not-so-good. It was trying to provide services back when we knew a lot less about disabilities. I think they did the best they could, given the times. Forgive them, forgive Mom and Dad, and forgive yourself for being scared. Just so you know, it definitely had an impact on me, too. Going there over the years, through junior high and high school, was when I first started to consider the ministry."

"You know, I've watched enough Masterpiece Theater to know the upper classes in Britain sent their sons off at a tender age to boarding schools, where they endured bullying, beatings, and…"

Bishop interrupts. "It was probably not as bad as you remember, and perhaps not as good as I like to think. Did you know Uncle Howard took Knight out of the state school for weekends and day trips all the time?"

"I had no idea."

"He was telling me the week before he died. Said they'd go to the zoo or the park. Sometimes to the warehouse, because Knight liked the forklifts and especially the Coke machine."

When Knight was sixty, he began behaving strangely. He refused to sit down. He would stand in the hallway at the group home for hours. He had bathroom accidents. After a lot of research and confusion, we figured out he was suffering from Alzheimer's. We learned it afflicts about twenty-five percent of adults with Down syndrome. It progressed quickly. Within a year, he faded and stopped eating and drinking. He died peacefully, with his favorite Christmas CD playing in the background.

"Bishop, when we parted at the airport last time I was here, you told me to get over myself."

"Hey, I didn't say…"

"No, not that exactly, but close enough. And you aren't wrong. I need your help. Your perspective. I'm ashamed to tell you that I've cried more about Sammie than about Michelle Hammond. I'm not trying to equate a dog's life with a person's life. Not at all. And I don't blame Campbell exactly, although he was an idiot and careless, which he agrees he was. I just keep going around and around in my mind over the same ground. I need an off-ramp."

"Have you been practicing your meditation? Praying?"

"The meditation is spotty, and I'm ashamed that my prayers are along the lines of gimme, gimme, gimme. *Let me find Sammie. Make Gary Hammond respond to my note. Let me see Max again.* My question is, 'Does God answer prayer?' People claim their child got well because of their prayers. Or someone's cancer disappeared because of prayer. Do you believe that?"

"Gosh Rook, you need to develop some small talk. On one of your visits, you asked about heaven, and now it's prayer." He smiles. "I have my opinion. Just remember that it's one humble minister's thoughts, not theological truth."

I sit up straight, eager to hear Bishop's ideas, but out of the corner of my eye, I notice a dog trotting down the sidewalk, alone. What's a dog doing here? I squint and try to make out if it's wearing a collar. I think of Sammie, suck in my breath, and concentrate on my brother.

"So, here it goes. Bishop's thoughts on prayer. God is our Father, right? But a perfect, loving parent, so far beyond our own experiences of parenting. Now remember back to Jay asking you for something, let's say he wanted to go to a party thrown by a senior and he was a freshman. He begged you. What would you say?"

Actually, that very thing had happened. We'd said no and had been punished for weeks with sulky silences.

"I'd say no. How's that relevant?"

"Stay with me. You tried to picture what might happen, and it all seemed bad—drinking, risk-taking, drugs, sex. Right?"

"Right."

"But what if instead of getting drunk, he'd met his future wife, or had a conversation that led him to his career choice. What I mean is, you did the best you could with what you knew, but your vision was limited. God's is unlimited."

I look for the stray dog and see it lifting its leg against a tree. Should I go out and try to catch it? Bishop continues.

"So he never interferes with the world, saving one kid and letting another die?"

"Do you really want God fixing everything according to our limited point-of-view? Do you think God saves a white Christian kid in Tulsa but allows hundreds of black kids in Africa—hell, in America—to die from bad water?" Bishop sounds angry. "I think God, our loving parent, hears our prayers, every single one, but the world he created keeps on spinning. There are diseases, accidents, natural disasters, and misguided, sick people who hurt others." His tone softens. "Prayer is just having a conversation with God."

Like Dr. Canon. Yes, talking with someone helps.

"I think conversations with God help us get clarity. We begin to understand ourselves, our feelings, what we ought to do. We learn to recognize God's voice. We feel stronger, more centered, more resilient. We may not get answers, but we may find meaning." Bishop twists in his seat to look at me. "We're not God. We can't see the big picture. We actually have no idea what we're asking for half the time."

Like my needlepoint. The backside is a dull mass of threads going every which way, but the front is a beautiful coherent image.

Bishop continues, "When we pray, we recognize that we are in need and that we aren't self-sufficient, but what *we* think we need, and what God knows we need, are not always in sync. That's why we say, in the Lord's Prayer, *thy* will be done."

Bishop is silent for a long time. Finally, he stirs and says, "The car accident might have a long-term effect you can't see. For example, perhaps in these past weeks, Michelle's husband found depths of understanding and love for her he never had before. Or he forged a relationship with God that will have a deep impact on the rest of his life. Or Michelle's children will grow up to be scientists or doctors who conduct amazing research on traumatic brain injury."

"That sounds like wishful thinking. Isn't it just as likely her husband and kids will be miserable?"

"Martin Luther King, Jr., said, 'The arc of the moral universe is long, but it bends toward justice.' We all—you, me, Michelle, Michelle's husband, her kids, Campbell—we're all just a tiny sliver of that arc. We can't see it, but it's bending toward justice, righteousness, peace, and mercy. Be content. God's in charge."

I sigh. "You certainly picked the right profession."

"Thanks, but it picked me. And if you want a shorthand version of all that, just remember Mom's verse from Romans 8:28. God works all things together for the good…"

"…of those who love him." I finish automatically. "It still seems complicated."

"No, it's simple. Trust and obey. Love your neighbor. Remember what the Buddhists say: Before Enlightenment, chop wood, carry water. After Enlightenment, chop wood, carry water."

"What the devil is that supposed to mean?"

"It means, sister dear, that we need to do the hard work of living and loving every day, regardless of our level of understanding." Bishop smiles. "I can tell you one prayer that will always be answered with a *Yes* from God."

"Now I'm curious. What is it?"

"Dear Father, can I grow closer to you?"

I'm relieved to see a man exit a nearby car and call the errant dog, who streaks toward the door he holds open. "Thanks. That actually helped. And thanks for letting me stay here for a few days."

"Sis, any time. I hated to see 'Operation Down the Field' end because we wouldn't be hanging out anymore."

"I didn't know you'd given our mission a name. I have to

admit, that's one good thing that's happened in the past few weeks. There've been no repercussions? No midnight knock on the door? No enraged alumni with pitchforks?"

"No, all is quiet on the fifty-yard line. Although if we do go to jail, I was thinking we could pass the time playing chess by mail."

"Umm…" I say while making a thumbs-down gesture.

I relax into the moment. The lost dog I just saw wasn't really lost, Uncle Howard is safely scattered, and my brother and I are on good terms. Our plan was crazy, but we pulled it off. It's time to turn my attention to my next assignment.

Visiting Mom and Dad.

to do list

- Have it out with Mom
- and Dad
- Thank C for earrings
- Stop feeling sorry for
- Rook
-
-
-
-
-
-
-

CHAPTER FIFTY

October

Reunion

T he names on the headstones fascinate me.

I walk among the grave markers of Crestline Cemetery, stopping when an inscription or statue catches my
eye. I do the math, feel a pang only when death found an
infant or a toddler. *Reuben Waits b.1923, d.1924 Gone to the
Angels.* I wonder where Irene's brother Willy is buried.

If I see a Bertha or a Clarence, I know without looking
that the person resting there was born long ago. I went
through school with Susans, Judiths,, and Davids. My Dad's
school roster was probably full of Arthurs, Ruths, and Freds. I
imagine Max's friends will be Madisons, Logans, and Baileys.
I stop short in front of one marker. *Jack Warner, b.1927,
d.2002.* I imagine little Jack in grade school with the other
kids chanting, "Little Jack Warner, sat in a corner..." I'm

amazed at what parents name their children. Do they say the whole name together out loud to see how it sounds? Do they consider how a name can be twisted and mocked?

I'm intrigued by the modern custom of couples hyphenating their last names when they marry. I wonder what happens when, on down the line, children of those kinds of unions get married, and they each have a hyphenated last name. Do they combine them all and have four last names? *Mr. and Mrs. Haisley-Haverstock are pleased to announce that their daughter Jennifer was married on April 16 to John Rutherford-Beckworth. The new Mr. and Mrs. Haisley-Haverstock-Rutherford-Beckworth will be honeymooning in France. Or perhaps opening a law firm.*

Arriving at the Brownlee plots, I arrange the camping blanket and thermos of coffee I've brought from Bishop's house. I fix my nest so that I can look directly at my parents' and Knight's graves. The day is overcast, with occasional drizzle, but not unpleasant. I pour some coffee and settle in.

"Hi, Mom and Dad. Hi, Knight. Rook here, come for a visit. Well, if I'm honest, it might be more like a confrontation. I've been having a hard time lately and spreading it around to my loved ones. Bishop and I are still tight, and he's been patient and helpful. The perfect big brother."

I sit, sipping, listening to the birds and squirrels. *If I were a squirrel, this would be a pretty cool place to live. Not much traffic, nice big trees, no dogs.* That makes me think of Sammie, and my throat tightens. "Campbell lost my dog, and an acquaintance died unexpectedly. Well, she wasn't really an acquaintance, but we had a connection. Campbell and I have been arguing a lot. I hurt Max, and Jay has banned me from his life. There, that's the whole sad story. Pretty messed up, huh?"

Off in the distance, I hear a lawnmower. Some leaves drift down, reminding me that summer is long over. I haven't seen Max in, what? I count on my fingers. *Nine weeks? No, ten.* I turn back to the headstones.

"I'm here because I'm upset about you putting Knight in the state school. Upset is probably a mild term. I'm angry. I don't understand why you did that. It really did a number on me, personality-wise. Helped make me a rule-following control freak. I can only imagine what it did to Knight. Abandoned—a child's worst nightmare. Why did you do it?"

There's no immediate answer, so I drift, recalling scenes from my childhood. Going to the state fair. Holidays and birthdays. My mother's apple pie. I picture myself as a baby, in a bassinet, with my two older brothers nearby. "Why are you picturing that?" asks Dr. Canon, who's taken up permanent residence in my head. *Duh. No need for a psychiatry degree for that one, Herr Doktor*, I tell him. *Because I was safe and innocent, and it was before—the event.*

"I guess it always comes down to this," I tell my parents. "The original relationship: parents and child, or more specifically, mother and child." I look at my mother's side of the headstone and conjure up an image of her sitting in an armchair, hemming a pair of Bishop's pants. "Sorry, Mom. Mothers generally have to take the rap. It's unfair but primeval."

I stand up and take a quick lap around the area to warm up and gather my thoughts. In the far distance, I see a tent, and a small backhoe at work, digging a grave. I return to my spot.

"Mom, I have no idea how it was for you, deciding to put Knight in the state school. It must have been terrible, and the pressure on you—I can't imagine. Still, according to my therapist, I've been blaming you for years. Guilt, blame, and shame. Talk about a trifecta. I've been holding a grudge, and believe me, I have a special talent for that."

I stop, take a deep breath, and plunge ahead.

"I get that it was tough. It wasn't like you could go online and look up answers, or join a support group, or look into the future. Bishop told me that your minister, of all people, joined forces with Dad to convince you to give Knight up. But why Mom? Talk to me."

My mother, busy with her sewing, listens and nods. She doesn't seem upset that her daughter is unloading on her. When she speaks, it's low but strong. *I loved Knight, honey. Don't ever think I didn't. Giving him up was the hardest sacrifice I ever made in my life.*

"Sacrifice? I don't understand."

I knew we couldn't give your brother what he needed. He needed special classes, and therapy, and the acceptance and understanding that our little town didn't have for children with disabilities. Rook, for heaven's sake, most people still called children with Down syndrome "Mongoloids" back then. I knew that if he stayed with us, he'd never grow up, in a sense. The local school couldn't accommodate him. And it would have made a huge impact on you and Bishop. After Dad and I were gone, it would have fallen on the two of you to take care of your brother. So I had to give up a child I loved so that he could have what we couldn't give him.

"But we could have given him love. A home. A family."

Mom is crying now, a little. *We still gave him that, honey. He just had two families—one with us, and one at the school. And later on, one at the group home. Oh Rook, I may be fooling myself. I don't know if it was the right thing. I just trusted God to make it come out all right in the end. I'm sorry it affected you. I tried to do the best I could.*

She pulls a small embroidered handkerchief out of her sleeve. Holds it to her eyes.

Compassion and love overwhelm me. I long to take my mother in my arms and hug her, bury my face in her neck, and inhale her Estée Lauder perfume. Two women, mother and daughter, joined by love, tragedy, faith, and a driving urge to do right. My judgments dry up and turn to dust. My heart feels scoured. Renewed.

"Mom, remember when you'd sing to me while swinging on the porch swing? That's one of my favorite memories. *Little Dog Under the Wagon. Over in the Meadow. Two Little Girls.* What a happy, safe cocoon: me there in my PJs, nestled close to you. Or when you read to me? *Charlotte's Web. The Wizard of Oz.*"

The illustrations from that long-ago book spring up in front of me. Dorothy and her friends skipping on the yellow brick road. The spires of Oz gleaming in the distance. Toto pulling back the curtain to reveal that the great Wizard is nothing more than a huckster from Kansas. Dorothy finding the courage to confront and defeat the wicked witch.

In the classic movie made from the book, there's a famous scene in which the Wicked Witch of the West spells out in the sky, in green smoke billowing from her broomstick, an ominous threat:

SURRENDER
DOROTHY

Surrender.

Campbell would point out it's the first step to recovery. Admit you're powerless. Let go. Seek help. I turn back to my mother.

"Maybe, like Dorothy, I've been trying all my life to get back home. Back to that porch swing. It's been a long detour, but I guess I had the power within me all along. I don't have ruby slippers, but I have friends, faith, and family. It's all I need."

I glance at my father's headstone. He's characteristically quiet. Leaving the kids to my mother while he reads the paper or listens to a baseball game. I enjoyed my time with him though. I'd spend an hour by his side in his workshop, handing him hammers and screwdrivers with the precision and speed of a surgical nurse. My reward would be a few random sentences. It was enough. He taught me everything I needed to know about commitment, integrity, and how to measure twice, cut once.

After a long time, I speak again. "Mom and Dad, I've been getting lots of signals from the universe that the key to all this is forgiveness and grace, so that's why I'm here. To ask your forgiveness for being a hardhearted, critical child, and for blaming you for the shitty deal you got."

And…?, my mother prompts, looking at me with love.

"And to forgive you, for what you did, for what you and Dad did, and how it affected me."

My mother smiles. *We love you, Rook. And don't say 'shitty.'*

I laugh, then cry. Slumped against my mother's headstone, my tiny frozen heart thaws a little, and for the first time in weeks, I feel a flicker of hope.

I look across the field of stone markers and see a second car parked near mine. A figure stands near it and starts walking toward me. The gait is familiar. Bishop? Barb? I feel a stab of fear. Jay? Has he come to tell me that Campbell is hurt?

"Hello," the figure says, and suddenly it's Campbell. I throw myself into his arms as our voices overlap each other.

"Why are you here?"

"Are you cold?"

"How did you know where I was?"

"I'm so glad to see you."

"I'm a jerk."

"I've been impossible."

And finally, together.

"I love you."

to do list

- <u>Try life without a list?</u>
-
-
-
-
-
-
-
-
-
-
-

CHAPTER FIFTY-ONE

October

Reconciled

We hold hands.

Walking to where the cars are parked, I take Campbell's hand, and his fingers close around mine. *Safety.* I've been slogging a lonely path these past weeks, and I can't remember why I made that choice. He was there all along, wanting to help.

We sit in Campbell's rental car, watching the leaves drift down. The silence holds no tension. I break it at last and say, "I'm glad you're here. The weeks since the accident have been... difficult. I've been difficult. I'm sure it's been confusing, watching me..." I shrug, not sure of the best word to describe my disintegration.

"I'm ashamed of how I've acted. You needed me and I failed. All I can say is how sorry I am, and that I want to do better. But then, there's Sammie."

My heart does something odd in my chest. I bite my lip and turn to study the passenger side mirror. *Sammie.*

"I'd give anything to get her back."

I turn to Campbell, and summon my better angels. "I know that. I know you're sorry, and that it was unintended. It'll be all right. I miss her, but what's most important to me is you." Saying these words, I realize they're true, and a weight lifts from my heart.

Campbell reaches out, squeezes my hand, and gives me a sad smile. "Thank you."

I read and reread the faint word inscribed on the dashboard: airbags. *That's what I need—something to inflate when I'm careening forward, and protect me from harm.*

"Why did you come here today?" Campbell's voice is warm but curious.

"I needed to talk to my parents. Get closure. Gosh, that sounds trite. But for the first time, I understand why people prefer burial over cremation, the headstones, and all that. It's a good place to visit. Talking to an urn on the mantle wouldn't have been as satisfying."

"Did it work?"

"Let's say I made progress. Rook McFadden—under construction. But I think the foundation is solid, so don't give up on me."

Campbell adjusts his seat so he can stretch his legs. "I learned a little from my secretary about the Hammonds. Michelle's mother has moved in with Gary and the kids to help out. All indicators are that Michelle got confused and took the pain and sleeping pills by accident."

"Still, I'm part of the chain of events that led to that happening. How do I live with that?"

"Like every human. One day at a time."

"Good old AA."

"Yes, it's the advice that fits almost every situation. In fact, my coming here to Ohio was AA inspired."

"It was?"

"I was at a meeting and had an idea about us, about how I should stop suggesting ways for you to change, and just work my own program. Listen without judgment. I do that in meetings, but not with you."

I've never been to an actual AA meeting. I've seen them depicted in movies and on TV, and I did attend Al-Anon for a year or so when Campbell first stopped drinking. Campbell is careful to preserve the sanctity of the meetings he goes to and the anonymity of those attending. I respect that and never pry. Occasionally, he'll share a joke or snippet of wisdom, and I always value those glimpses into that part of his life.

"Rook, you were right on the trail, when we fought about the money. I owe you, and I should feel nothing but gratitude for the life we have together. A guy the other day said that living with an alcoholic is like rolling around in broken glass. I thought that was good. And you did that. You rolled in that glass for the ten years I was actively drinking, and you're still living with an alcoholic. A recovered one, sure, but an alcoholic all the same. I may get the AA anniversary chips, but you should get a medal."

His words hang there, and for once, he gives me not only seven seconds to respond, but twice that. "I'll decline the medal, but thank you. It's been worth it. *You're* worth it."

"*We're* worth it. Campbell smiles and points to the earrings I'm wearing. His gift. "Do you like them? They look great."

"I love them. I'm sorry I spoiled the presentation."

He waves this away. "We've both been doing and saying hurtful things for a while now, and I know we'll fall back into our old, bad habits without some help. I guess I'm saying we should probably go to counseling together, either to Dr. Canon, or somebody else."

I nod, full of gratitude. "That's a good suggestion."

We're silent again. I turn toward Campbell. "Do you think we'll ever find a smooth road? It seems like it's just one bump after another."

"Being married is hard. We went on auto-pilot, and that doesn't work. Rook, I love you. You're my best friend and I think you're beautiful, and smart, and ... there's nobody I'd rather argue with than you." He smiles. "Shall we go home now? To Colorado?"

"Yes. Let's go home. I want to try these new wings."

"I took today and Monday off school. Family emergency. We can spend the weekend here if you want." He pauses, unsure. "I have an idea."

"What's that?"

"I thought it'd be amazing to go the OSU-Purdue game tomorrow and check out your uncle's final resting place. Bishop said he could get four mediocre seats since it's not a major game. Be fun to see the band, script Ohio, the whole deal."

"You flew all the way here to put Humpty Dumpty Rook back together, so yes, I want to go to the OSU game with you. It's a great idea."

He leans over the console and grabs my hands. "For once, I don't care if the Buckeyes win or lose. They'll win, of course, but there's only one thing I want."

"What's that?"
"Being there with you."

to do list

- Hang on, Sloopy
- Go, Bucks, Go!
- Practice gratitude
-
-
-
-
-
-
-
-
-

CHAPTER FIFTY-TWO

October

Progress

The OSU campus is a zoo.

The ten blocks surrounding the stadium are packed and throbbing with excitement. We get to campus early, pay $20 to park in a convenience store lot, and walk a mile south on High Street, marveling at the crowd. A car drives by with a mannequin dressed in Purdue colors tied to the front bumper. A student leans against an apartment building smoking a joint. A dozen more are mashed together on the front porch, drinking and laughing.

As we near the Horseshoe, the crowd increases. Most sport the scarlet and gray of Buckeye country. They stream toward parking lots filled with food trucks, tents, and tailgaters. Music blares. Vendors hawk T-shirts, sweatshirts, and hats. I smell brats, popcorn, pizza. Cops wearing orange vests try to keep the mass of humanity on the sidewalks. Every restaurant is overflowing. It's Mardi Gras, the Macy's Thanksgiving Parade, Times Square on New Year's Eve, the Super Bowl, and the World Series all rolled into one. Fans and onlookers are here to party.

We find ourselves near St. John's Arena. "Hey," Barb says. "Let's go in and watch the Skull Session." Skull Sessions are pep rallies held two hours before the game. Walking inside the cavernous space, we join 10,000 fans to witness the electrifying arrival of the band, who come strutting in to a fast cadence of drum beats and play all the fan favorites. The football team, dressed in suits and ties, makes a brief appearance, but it's the band that holds center stage.

Campbell taps his watch. "Let's go see some football, people!"

The stadium feels familiar after my two recent visits, and we climb to our seats and settle in. I turn to the field and study the line markings.

"Bishop, those lines look perfect, right?"

He considers the lines and agrees, "Those lines are, without a doubt, the most beautiful and excellent lines I have ever seen."

Ohio Stadium is filling up. "Anybody want something from the concession stand?" Bishop asks. "I'm getting a slice of pizza before the pre-game."

Campbell says, "That reminds me. One of my teachers gave me a recipe for chocolate chip cookies she says works at high altitudes. I promise to eat the failures because that's just the kind of guy I am." *Huh.* One of my bucket list items. This day is getting better and better.

The crowd stirs. Heads are turning, shoulders straightening, eyes fixing on a concrete ramp running from inside the stadium to the field. The announcer's voice booms: "Ladies and Gentlemen, the pride of the Buckeyes, The Ohio State University Marching Band!"

The band high-steps its way onto the field, executing their famous ramp entrance. A moment later, the drum major struts to the front and bends backward until the tip of his plume touches the field. A roar shakes the air. Then, brass horns blazing and drums crackling, the band sweeps down the field, the drum major keeping time with his baton in that aggressive thrusting motion perfected in the 1930s. A thrilling spectacle executed with precision and authority, which the crowd rewards with a crescendo of screaming.

Then an interlude of quiet, while the band plays, and the crowd sings the OSU alma mater. More quick-stepping, and to the rhythmic clapping of thousands of hands, the band gives the people the spectacle they've made famous: Script Ohio. The formation's thrilling climax, the dotting of the *i*, is a coveted role reserved for fourth and fifth year sousaphone players. Only a handful of exceptions have been made: Bob Hope, astronaut John Glenn, and few lucky others.

I read an interesting bit from the field of handwriting analysis about the origin of the dot over an *i* (so that it can be distinguished from a *u*) and what the placement of it says about the person doing the dotting. These experts see a link between the precise placing of the dot and the attention, precision, memory, and concentration of the writer.

I'm a confirmed *i* dotter myself. It's *my* signature move, So I watch with longing as the *i* in Ohio gets its finishing touch. The Hammond family, Michelle in particular, Max, Sammie, Knight: each one represents a huge un-dotted i in my life, something I can't fix, perfect, finish, or control. I have to accept what I cannot change. Change what I can. Seek the wisdom to know the difference. The Serenity Prayer. The only prayer I need.

The band now forms a wide channel, and the football team and staff run onto the field, proceeded by Brutus, the famous mascot, waving a huge Buckeye flag.

"And that's just the pre-game!" Barb leans over to comment.

Band personnel put up a ladder midfield, and the director climbs it to lead the national anthem. Everyone stands, hats off, hands clasped to hearts, as the words are rendered by the largest choir I've ever heard. The stars and stripes whip in the wind, the sun makes an appearance, and the spectacle is hitting every sense. You can smell the popcorn and hot chocolate, feel the wind off the river, hear the dying strains of that beautiful anthem, taste the hazy smoke and drift of fall leaves, and see the predominance of red attire in the stands in contrast to the black and white band uniforms on the green field of battle.

The first quarter begins. I try to follow the game but can't settle my mind. Players trot on and off the field; fans cheer, boo, stamp their feet, scream; the referees confer and throw down flags as penalties are called. There are long moments when nothing seems to happen. I resolve to keep my eye on the football, but it's like watching a master magician. I glue my eyes on the quarterback's hands when suddenly a player streaks down the field with the ball tucked up under *his* arm.

I'm baffled by the names of the players' positions. Growing up, I knew there were tackles, guards, ends, centers, quarterbacks, halfbacks, and fullbacks. Those names appealed to my logical and spatially oriented brain. Now there are cornerbacks, safeties, outside linebackers, inside linebackers, strong safeties, free safeties, running backs, tight ends, wide receivers, and on and on. I'm seriously uninformed.

The half ends with the Buckeyes leading seventeen to ten. The crowd is delirious and hungry, and many push toward the restrooms and concession stands. Most remain for what is arguably the best spectacle of the afternoon: the halftime show put on by TBDBITL.

Campbell taps me, and I turn to him. He's holding two pieces of paper that he's torn from a corner of the program and offers me one. "I want you to write down the dollar amount you'd like to give the Hammonds, and I'll do the same. Then we'll compare." He gives me a pen.

I'm puzzled at his timing but take the pen and consider where I stand. I think about my sessions with Dr. Canon, about Rev. Leatherman, my talks with Bishop, my praying and meditating, my visit to the Hammonds, Michelle's death, my time at Crestline Cemetery. I carefully print a number, fold the paper, and hand it to my husband. He does the same.

I unfold his paper. Read the number. It's larger than mine. I slip the paper in my pocket, kiss Campbell. "Thank you," I whisper.

He's about to respond when the announcer's voice takes on a new urgency. "And now fans, let's welcome to the field the Purdue University Marching Band!"

"What! We have to sit through another band's performance?"

But I sit back and enjoy the show, honoring America's armed services. The Purdue band is good, but they aren't TBDBITL. Finally, the air takes on an electrified quality. Like animals that can sense an approaching weather front, the crowd starts acting in unison. People return to their seats, conversations are cut off, heads turn toward the field. Again the announcer makes the iconic introduction: "Ladies and Gentlemen, The Pride of the Buckeyes, The Ohio State University Marching Band!"

The band marches onto the field and begins their show, a tribute to the conquest of outer space. It's brilliant. They form the Starship Enterprise, the Millennium Falcon, and a rocket ship. They depict a Purdue player falling into a black hole while the crowd screams in approval. They move and play with breathtaking professionalism, and the four of us watch with awe.

I remember the slogan in the practice room, facing the band members in bold black letters:

PICK UP YOUR FEET,
TURN YOUR CORNERS SQUARE
AND DRIVE, DRIVE, DRIVE!!!

Good advice for any endeavor.

After the game ends, we remain sitting. I'm not sure my legs will work. Then, to my surprise, with the stadium almost empty, the OSU band marches onto the field. They traverse from end zone to end zone, playing several numbers and looking just as crisp and flawless as they had at halftime, then they disappear through a door in the wall.

Bishop stands and addresses the deserted field. "Uncle

Howard. We salute you. We admire and respect you. You served your country and built a business. You cared about and strengthened your community. You loved your family. You stood on your principles. You created a lot of laughter in the world. You really were a member of The Greatest Generation. We are honored to have fulfilled your last request and humbled that you chose us to do so. We will be good stewards of your money, and we hope you approve of your final resting place."

I stand up beside my brother. "I wanted to say a few words about Uncle Howard also. I wasn't sure how to top the professional here." I nod at Bishop. "But then I remembered something I read a few years ago and it seemed fitting. It goes like this: When you were born, you cried, and the people around you rejoiced. Live your life in such a way that when you die, the people around you will cry, and you'll rejoice. I think Howard lived his life like that."

"Bravo, Howard!"

to do list

- Pack for CO
- Live and let love
- Wait... upon the Lord (and
  Jay, and Carly)
-
-
-
-
-
-
-
-

CHAPTER FIFTY-THREE

October

Gratitude

I'm running on adrenaline.

Slumped in a pew for the Sunday service at Woodbridge Presbyterian, I'm giddy with relief and excitement. I can't even remember the second half of the football game. Ohio State won, I know that, but football was not a priority as my mind swirled with plans, ideas, and gratitude.

Now I'm in church, after a restless night, feeling sick and bleary. I try to focus on the sermon, but after a few minutes, I put my energy into keeping my eyes open. I don't disgrace myself and even manage to exchange pleasantries with the Abernathys at the coffee hour afterward.

For lunch, Barb makes turkey paninis, complete with cranberry sauce. A mini-Thanksgiving between two slices of sourdough. She's wearing an apron that asks

RV
EATING
YET?

"I'm an heiress, Bishop," I say. "I believe you should be serving my panini from a silver chafing dish."

Bishop snorts and shoves the sandwich platter across the table.

"Oh, and have the car brought around, will you?" I continue. "I think I'll visit the peasants after I dine."

"Yes milady," he says in a deep, butler-type voice. "Shall we schedule the beheadings before or after dinner?"

I snicker. It's good to be heading home, but I'll miss my brother.

After lunch, Campbell offers to pack while I take a walk to clear my head. There's a lot to think about. Campbell and I are talking again, without rancor or accusations. Last night, face-to-face in bed, we shared our fears and hopes. It was easy and natural, despite the long hiatus. The relief at coming back together and the comfort of being with my husband and lifelong friend brought a peace that had eluded me for weeks.

In the darkness, I reached out and took his hand. "I didn't realize how wound up I've been all summer and fall. I think I've been a little crazy."

"It's been a rough patch, for sure, and I'm not proud of my behavior either. I know this: when we're on the same side, we can handle whatever comes our way. Team McFadden."

"I like that. My solo act wasn't working out." I moved

into his arms. Campbell, my companion on The Yellow Brick Road of life, who, like all human beings, is a mix of strengths and weaknesses: anxious and courageous, scatter-brained and thoughtful, insensitive and tender. I'm a mix too, and the joy of our marriage is we can exhibit all these traits and find approval, or push-back when it's needed, but always—love.

Besides, would I ever find another husband who will willingly iron all my clothes?

I walk the streets of Bishop's neighborhood and my thoughts drift to Max. I was desperate to move close to him, intent on forging a relationship. After the accident, I was determined to re-enter his life. Now? I feel no tension or strain. *My* wants and needs have drained away. I will make a nest for him, and when the time is right, he will come and settle there, close to my heart.

What would Frank Brownlee think of me now? Am I strong? Brave? The revelation at Dr. Canon's office has helped. I love a well-balanced equation. Cause and effect. Action and reaction. Garbage in and garbage out. Childhood trauma and a screwed-up adult.

My childhood was not traumatic, I protest. *It was wonderful.*

As if summoned, Dr. Canon speaks in my head. "But you did experience a traumatic event. It was—"

I cut him off. "Let's not over-examine this, OK? Like Jay says, 'It is what it is. Deal.'" I shove Dr. Canon into a closet. "Thank you for your service. See you later. Bye-bye."

Why did I react to the Knight thing, but Bishop didn't? Am I such a tender flower? I don't like this line of thought. Maybe Bishop's wounds are deeply hidden, or his training and profession have given him the tools to deal with them. Or perhaps he blocks his emotions and spackles them over with kindness, understanding, and patience—like a good little minister.

It sounds like fodder for a future therapy session with Dr. Canon. *Ha, cannon fodder, that's a good one!* I take Dr. Canon out of the closet and dust him off. I'll go visit him again. I want to tell him about my visit to my parents, Bishop's thoughts about the state school, and the current status of my relationship with Campbell. He can even do his silent routine, a talent he's perfected. *Don't want to scare the horses*, I imagine one of his professors joking to a classroom full of earnest young psychiatry students. That's OK, I'll do the talking.

I'm not sure Dr. Canon is right for the joint counseling Campbell suggested, but we'll find someone. Warren Leatherman will have a recommendation. I realize I now consider Warren my pastor, hug myself, and smile.

Thinking of Dr. Canon reminds me of his assignment: breaking rules. So far I've managed to go through the Express Lane at the grocery, marked MAXIMUM 15 ITEMS, with eighteen items. I composed an email to an old college friend that contained an error. I deliberately put *its* instead of *it's*. I stared at that error—*Its been a while since we talked*—a full three minutes before I hit send. Consoled myself with the thought that maybe her grammar isn't up to speed and she won't notice.

I approach Bishop's house. The Ohio maples and oaks are blazing with color. Colorado offers a more monochrome fall with lots of yellow aspen trees. I miss the variety here but feel no regret about leaving and heading to Colorado. Home.

I'm eager to be patient. Now there's an oxymoron for you. I pick up the pace of my walk. My heart beats steadily, joyfully, at the prospect of going home. I'm ready to wait: for God, for Jay, for the answer to my prayers.

A grandmother and child reunion.

to do list

- Wrap up Max's stocking
- Offer to dog-sit for
-     neighbors
- Be still
- Be

CHAPTER FIFTY-FOUR

November

Transition

I see three nuggets among the dross.

I've walked up to the mailbox and I sort through the mail as I head home. I open an envelope from the CASA organization, read the letter, and smile. My application has been approved, and my training starts in four weeks. I'm going to become a Court Appointed Special Advocate and work within the court system to befriend an abused or neglected child and act as a champion for his or her rights. I'll use my logic, organizational skills, and assertiveness for a good cause.

Completing the mail trifecta is a letter from the law office of Buckner, Swanson & Cole, and a postcard from Bishop. I arrive back on the deck, and Campbell appears from the garage, where he's been vacuuming the cars' interiors. I show him the mail.

"Hey, I'll get lunch together while you read those to me." Campbell pulls lunchmeat, bread, fruit, cheese, and mustard from the refrigerator. I read the letter from Bernie Cole first.

November 5, 2008
Dear Rook,

Hello from Columbus! I hope you, Campbell, and your entire family are doing well.

The first annual Howard H. Rawlings Band Scholarships have been awarded. Lindsay Wheeler, a sophomore from Marietta, and Paul Lawrence, a freshman from Dayton, will each receive $5,000 for the spring semester at OSU. Lindsay plays the trombone, and Paul is a drummer. They're thrilled, and I'll send you copies of their gracious thank-you letters in my next mailing. The scholarship fund is structured and invested to ensure that annual scholarships will be awarded for many years to come. I've notified Bishop about these recipients as well.

I'm pleased with how quickly Howard's house sold. It's moving along nicely, and your proceeds should be available in about six weeks, after the close.

The annuity you asked me to set up for Gary Hammond will pay approximately $500 per month for five years. I'll contact him when all the paperwork is done, and as requested, keep it confidential and anonymous. The money will be automatically deposited to his checking account on the first of each month and should help Mr. Hammond provide the children with some extras— school activities and fees, family vacations, that type of thing. I'll keep in touch with them and give you periodic updates.

Walt McCaffey and his wife have scheduled their week-long, all-expenses-paid vacation to Hawaii for next March. I can assure you that they will enjoy every amenity, thanks to you and Bishop.

The Franklin County Group Home is over-the-moon about your $25,000 gift. They are choosing a contractor, and once the money clears, construction of the Knight Brownlee deck, screened porch, and gazebo will start. It should provide the ten residents and their caregivers a beautiful outdoor space. As you specified, the design will include a porch swing. They've invited you and your family to attend the ribbon-cutting, tentatively set for next May.

I'm in the process of setting up the 529 college plan you want for your grandson. The initial deposit, plus the regular monthly deposits you'll be making, should ensure he will graduate from college debt-free.

I believe I have followed my marching orders (haha) as you spelled them out.

Didn't this all turn out splendidly? Howard would have been delighted. He'd have applauded your ingenuity, laughed at your audaciousness, and cheered your use of the inheritance. In short, his money was well spent and will make a lasting impact on the people, and of course, that special institution, that he loved. Well done, Rook and Bishop!

If you come to Columbus in May, please get in touch. I'd love to take you to lunch and meet some more McFaddens. This whole endeavor has been a delightful change of pace from the usual stuffy wills and estates we deal with.

Naturally, I'll never watch another Buckeye football game or visit the Horseshoe without thinking of Howard and his fifty-yard line seat. Brilliant!

Thank you for letting me pick a couple of band mementos from Howard's collection. I'll enjoy having those in my office.

Sincerely yours,
Bernie Cole

I finish Bernie's letter and glance toward my office, picturing the Ohio memento that pleases me most—the small Buckeye Brands truck I first saw on Walt's desk. It's now on my bookshelf and carries a very special cargo: a pinch of Howard Rawlings's ashes.

"Well," Campbell says. "That's great. But it's a bummer that Gary Hammond doesn't know who's behind all the money. Are you sure you want it that way?"

"Yes. It's good for me not to take credit." I eat a sweet pickle and watch Campbell assemble sandwiches and heat water for tea. He nods toward the mail.

"Read Bishop's postcard."

I study the picture of the Grand Canyon on Bishop's postcard. Wonder if he rode a mule to the bottom. I turn it over and read:

Dear Rook,

This is our last trip in the current RV. When the money comes through, we're going to upgrade and live in style! We'll be coming your way in a couple of weeks so we'll stop and say hello. The big news is that I've been working on my book. Now that I can afford to self-publish, I've been quite motivated. See you soon.

Love, B.

P.S. Saw this on a church marquee near Flagstaff and thought of you: "To forgive is to set a prisoner free, and to realize the prisoner was you." Be free, sis.

My throat constricts. I go out on the deck and lean against the rail. I notice a small herd of mule deer straggling across the lower end of the meadow. Campbell comes up beside me and hands me a cup of tea. Together we watch the deer.

There are five, moving in a delicate ballet as they graze. They take turns lifting their heads and fanning their large ears back and forth, alert for predators but enjoying the moment—the sun, the grass, and the safety and closeness of their family members.

I sip my tea and lean into Campbell. There are five in my little family too. Later today I'll find out if we're still a unit, watching each other's backs, bound together in love.

We've been invited to Jay and Carly's for dinner.

I've finished Max's Christmas stocking. It's on the kitchen table in a sheath of acid-free tissue paper. I've stitched his name in red at the top, above the scenes of snowmen, Santas, and reindeer. It's large, with a white satin lining, red cording, and a loop at the top corner so that he can *hang it on the chimney with care.* Every stitch a prayer. I've designed a secret interior pocket in the lining where I can tuck notes, money, or special treats. I'll present it to him later today. *Will he remember me? Shy away? Run into my arms?*

Campbell drinks his tea and gives me a squeeze. "Hey, it's nippy out here." He reads my thoughts. "Are you nervous about today?"

I start to answer, then stop. Breathe. Apply Dr. Canon's techniques. No jokes. Honest emotions. "I am nervous about it. I want to grab him, hug him, and make a big deal of his stocking, but I imagine full-on grandmother mode is not the way to go."

"I get that you're nervous. Kids are tough, though. They get over stuff."

I think about Knight and my own childhood. Sometimes the wounds go deep.

Campbell continues, "Jay and Carly asked us to come. Isn't that what we've been hoping for? Max is talking more, acting like his old self. The doctors agree that time will do its work." *The doctors: Orthopedic surgeons. Child psychologists. Trauma specialists.* I bite my lip.

"That breaks my heart. Max seeing all those doctors because of me. Me seeing a psychiatrist because of me. The Hammonds." I hear the judgment in my tone and pause. "OK, let me try that again." Learning to catch myself in mid-rant and choosing a different path is hard work. I fail multiple times a day. "I'm sad the accident hurt so many people. I'm grateful to you for hanging in there." I move closer to Campbell and slip my arms around him.

We watch the deer for a few minutes. I think about the legal case, which I've dubbed The Never-Ending Story. I can't control it, so I need to let it go. More hard work and daily failure. *Muscles grow stronger with exercise. Habits grow stronger with repetition. Let go. Rinse. Repeat.*

"He's going to love that stocking. It's beautiful."

"He's two. I doubt he even notices it."

"It's something he'll have all his life—an heirloom. When he's ninety years old, he'll be sitting with his great-grandchildren around the Christmas tree, and he'll look at that stocking and think of his Gram. How much she loved him, and how much he loved her."

"I do love him. I hope it's natural. Like before."

The planet teeters off-balance, straining to find a new orbit. Today I find out if we can resume our natural places in the McFadden Galaxy, or instead go spinning out into space.

Separate and alone.

to do list

- Keep calm
- Carry on
- Hope
-
-
-
-
-
-
-
-
-

CHAPTER FIFTY-FIVE

November

Invitation

I watch Max from the hallway.

In the family room, my grandson has built an impressive train of chairs, cardboard boxes, stuffed animals, and toy trucks and cars. He wears his engineer's hat and has colored strips of construction paper tickets in one hand and a whistle in the other. He's playing the role of conductor, engineer, fireman, brakeman, porter, and passenger. "Train," he announces, and I thrill to his voice.

Jay had met us at the door, holding it open as I led the way up the walk, Campbell behind me, carrying Max's stocking. "Welcome to the railroad yard," Jay says. As I pass, my son touches me lightly on the arm. "Mom. It's good to see you." Carly waves from the kitchen.

I hang back as Jay resumes his role: He's a bear attacking

the train, and Max runs from car to car, helping his passengers, who are a motley bunch. I see all his favorite stuffies: Giraffey, Blue Monkey, Seal, Elfey, and a dozen others. Finally Jay the Bear is beaten back and retreats to the kitchen to help Carly make coffee. Campbell and I watch Max move from car to car, muttering to his passengers. As he turns, we see the shirt he's wearing. **World's Best Big Brother.**

For about ten seconds I assume Carly bought the shirt at a consignment shop without paying attention to the message, then the light bulb goes off. I go into the kitchen, eyes wide.

"Max's shirt? Does that mean? Are you?" Campbell and I swivel our heads back and forth between Jay and Carly, who nod and grin. I put my arms out, and my daughter-in-law comes to me. Campbell hugs Jay, then we switch. The McFadden Galaxy is adding a previously undiscovered planet.

"When is this fabulous baby due? How do you feel? Is Max excited? Do you know if it's a boy or a girl?"

Carly smiles. "The baby is due next May, and we don't know the sex. I feel great. We haven't told Max because we knew he'd spill the beans about a baby 'brudder' or 'sisser.' We wanted this moment to be the huge reveal."

Another grandchild. I'd never been able to have a second baby, so this is a blessing indeed. I remember a quote attributed to Julian of Norwich, a famous 14th-century mystic: *All shall be well, and all shall be well, and all manner of thing shall be well.*

"Why don't you go play train with Max while we get some snacks together?" Jay sounds casual, but it's like receiving a gilt-edged invitation on creamy, heavy stationery. You know it's important. I'm not sure why we've come back together so effortlessly today. *Because of my therapy? Their therapy? God? Prayer? Tears? Time?* Whatever it is, I'm going to accept the invitation and not question why I've been included.

Campbell stays in the kitchen. *Go time.* I sit on a low bench near the fireplace. "Hi, Max," I say. "I like your train."

He regards me with a seriousness appropriate to the moment. I search his face for signs of trauma and see a faint scar near his ear. Before I can stop myself, I send a prayer up: *Lord, please let this little boy be unmarked by the accident, both inside and outside.* I watch my prayer drift upward, then, with a sigh, snatch it back. I substitute a different petition, one that Bishop would approve. *Lord, help me be the best possible grandmother to this child, regardless of what life holds.*

Max is pleased to have a human passenger and directs me to climb aboard. I fold myself into a cardboard box, where my seatmates, a panda and a stormtrooper, have struck up a détente. With Max at the wheel, our train rolls out. Remembering Campbell's remark on the deck, I picture Max as an old man. I'm a memory, and the accident is a digital record in the archives of the insurance company. The epiphany that follows is small, but enough. There's only one "To Do" that matters.

*Give thanks for each God-given moment
of grace I encounter*

Max jumps out of the engine and, as the conductor, visits each car. He gives me a small smile as I stretch out my hand, palm up. He extracts a piece of pale blue construction paper from his pocket and gives me the only thing I need.

A ticket to ride.

Thanks for reading *Rook Makes A Move*.
If you enjoyed it, please consider posting a candid review
on Goodreads or wherever you enjoy buying,
discussing, or discovering new books.

AUTHOR'S NOTE

T he character of Rook McFadden popped into my head one August morning in 2014 as I was taking a walk. I went home and started writing. I was retired, a new grandmother, and as a first-time novelist, I had no idea I was embarking on a six-year journey.

Although the story has gone through many iterations, one constant has been stellar advice from the professionals I've consulted along the way. I want to thank Jason Fleming, Chase Milburn, Trooper Josh Lewis, Chris O'Dell, Erika Krouse, Mark Springer, Doug Kurtz, Lisa Kilrow, Dent Rhodes, Nora Esthimer, Tara Groth, Lyn Hawks, Anna Pitoniak, and April Williams for their counsel and expertise.

I'm grateful to the Lighthouse Writers Workshop in Denver and to the North Carolina Writers' Network, which provided invaluable resources and contacts.

Thanks to Ed Hashek, Bruce Stahly, Allan and Mary K. Horton, Annie Hutt, and Michelle Beaglehole, who read early drafts of the book and offered kind, insightful comments.

As I neared the end, another group of advisers emerged. Chief Ronnie Price, Dr. John Hale, Dr. Bill Rosenfeld, Dr. Andrew Rosenfeld, and Howard Fifer gave excellent guidance on car accidents, first responders, medical matters, legal considerations, and insurance issues. A shout out also to the TBDBITL Alumni Club, Inc. for their assistance.

The turning point for the book was my meeting Steve Peha in March 2019. Steve became my editor and friend. He challenged me to produce better writing and offered sharp suggestions, but more importantly, he understood Rook in a deep and sympathetic way that made our conversations a joy. Thank you, Steve.

Other amazing folks in my corner: Victoria Colotta, from VMC Art & Design, designed the cover and interior of the book and did a first-rate line edit. Andrew Taylor-Troutman provided feedback, cheers, and prayers, and Nancy Dorato and her Pinehurst Book Club graciously read and commented on one of the later drafts.

I salute bestselling author Anna Quindlen, whom I was lucky enough to meet in the spring of 2018. She read part of the manuscript, liked it, and offered words of encouragement and valuable referrals to me, a virtual stranger, simply out of the goodness of her heart.

My son Ben Hilliard and my daughter-in-law Casey have read every version of the book and said they liked them all. That's love. I thank my siblings—Marilyn Mendelson, Martha Lee Thatcher, David McKenzie, and Mike McKenzie, plus my sister-in-law Beth Orr—and their families, who have rooted for me all these years.

To my husband of fifty years, David, who has listened to my rants, laughed at my jokes, read the book countless times, and offered spot-on critiques, I award a lifetime, paid-in-full marriage bank account (see chapter 22).

Sharp-eyed readers will find inconsistencies, discrepancies, and errors in these pages. I could pretend, as Rook does in chapter 53, that I put them in deliberately, to counter my perfectionism, but the truth is that all errors are mine only and were inadvertent.

I can trace the inspiration for this book to the birth of my first grandson, Theo. Two years later, he was joined by brother Quincy, and together, these two boys are my sunshine. I'm blessed that they and their parents live nearby, and I can see them often. I hope they will recognize this book as a testimony of my love for them. May it be so.

Cynthia Hilliard
Chapel Hill, NC
June 2020

ABOUT THE AUTHOR

C ynthia Hilliard lives near Chapel Hill, NC, with her husband, David, and dog, Lola. Her grandchildren, and their parents, live close by. *Rook Makes A Move* is her first novel.

Visit www.cynthiahilliard.com to find a list of discussion questions designed for book clubs and to learn more about the author.

Made in United States
Orlando, FL
12 January 2022

13369054R00209